D0394712

WITHDRAWN

TWENTIETH CENTURY VIEWS

The aim of this series is to present the best in contemporary critical opinion on major authors, providing a twentieth century perspective on their changing status in an era of profound revaluation.

Maynard Mack, *Series Editor*
Yale University

BENJAMIN FRANKLIN

BENJAMIN FRANKLIN

A COLLECTION OF CRITICAL ESSAYS

Edited by

Brian M. Barbour

Cap. a

Prentice-Hall, Inc. A SPECTRUM BOOK *Englewood Cliffs, N.J.*

Library of Congress Cataloging in Publication Data

MAIN ENTRY UNDER TITLE:

Benjamin Franklin: a collection of critical essays.

(Twentieth Century Views) (A Spectrum Book)
  Bibliography: p.
  1. Franklin, Benjamin, 1706-1790—Literary art—Addresses, essays, lectures.   2. Franklin, Benjamin, 1706-1790. The Autobiography—Addresses, essays, lectures.
3. American literature—Colonial period, ca. 1600-1775—History and criticism—Addresses, essays, lectures.
4. American literature—1783-1850—History and criticism—Addresses, essays, lectures.   I. Barbour, Brian M.
E302.6.F8B46   973.3'092'4   79-12443
ISBN 0-13-074856-0
ISBN 0-13-074849-8 pbk.

Editorial/production supervision by Heath Silberfeld
Cover illustration by Stanley Wyatt
Manufacturing buyer: Cathie Lenard

10   9   8   7   6   5   4   3   2   1

PRENTICE-HALL INTERNATIONAL, INC. *(London)*
PRENTICE-HALL OF AUSTRALIA PTY. LIMITED *(Sydney)*
PRENTICE-HALL OF CANADA, LTD. *(Toronto)*
PRENTICE-HALL OF INDIA PRIVATE LIMITED *(New Delhi)*
PRENTICE-HALL OF JAPAN, INC. *(Tokyo)*
PRENTICE-HALL OF SOUTHEAST ASIA PTE. LTD. *(Singapore)*
WHITEHALL BOOKS LIMITED *(Wellington, New Zealand)*

Contents

For
René Fortin
and for
Steve Clark and Ralph Martin

Introduction: Franklin, Lawrence, and Tradition

by Brian M. Barbour

I

Modern criticism of Benjamin Franklin as a writer and moralist revolves around D.H. Lawrence's famous essay in *Studies in Classic American Literature*. In that essay Lawrence directly challenged Franklinian themes and values that American creative writers had been quarreling with, more obliquely, for at least a century. For them, as for Lawrence, Franklin seemed to define inadequately the center of the American experience, and their spirited resistance to him helped forge a central tradition of American literature. What is at issue here, it is important to note, is not the historical Franklin; it is the vision of life that he so memorably articulated and to which he deliberately lent his enormous prestige. This outlook, presented in the *Autobiography* and in a handful of congruent essays (e.g., "Advice to a Young Tradesman," "The Way to Wealth"), gradually became a normative ethos—defining values and ideals, molding sensibility—in American culture. Given strength by a century and a half of secularization, it codified the sense of the opportunity offered by the new American experience in predominantly economic terms, and it was resistance to this code that energized many of the greatest American writers. In Franklin, and what was made of him, we see the decisive connection of American literature with the wider social experience.

Although Jonathan Edwards gives us a historical alternative to Franklin, it is with Emerson that conscious resistance to the

Franklinians and their scheme of values becomes a major literary theme. The continuous design of Emerson's writing was to wrest the American dream away from them and redefine the American opportunity in moral and spiritual terms: "The one thing in the world, of value, is the active soul." The whole of his thought is concentrated in that single sentence with its radical challenge to materialist assumptions. What he saw and feared in the Franklinian outlook was not just acquisitiveness but moral complacency, a satisfaction with the ordinary self, apparently validated by economic achievement. Hence his effort to redefine self-reliance. Both men extolled self-reliance as a cardinal virtue, but where Franklin's self-reliance was a drive for power by the self-assertive conscious will, Emerson's was an exploratory search for self-knowledge by the moral will.

Thoreau also challenged Franklinian materialism. In the *Autobiography* Franklin was concerned to teach the means to material success; its worth as a goal he took for granted:

> Having emerg'd from the Poverty and Obscurity in which I was born and bred, to a State of Affluence and some Degree of Reputation in the World, and having gone so far thro' Life with a considerable Share of Felicity, the conducing Means I made use of, which, with the Blessing of God, so well succeeded, my Posterity may like to know, as they may find some of them suitable to their own Situations, and therefore fit to be imitated.[1]

Thoreau recoiled sharply from these notions. Such concern with *means* to the virtual dismissal of *ends,* such emphasis on imitation or conformity, as well as the satisfied reluctance to explore the relation of *having* to *being*—these appalled him: he diagnosed such a life as "not life," but a mere prolongation of physical processes without spiritual purpose or sense of a deeper reality. Hence he begins *Walden* with an all-out satirical attack under the name of "Economy." There he aims to destroy the false economy that results in a mere accumulation of goods, and substitute for it a true economy, focusing life toward a spiritual end, a reality not eroded by time. Through his title, his lists, his witty handling of asceticism, and his structure ("Economy" is a parody of the

---

[1]*The Autobiography of Benjamin Franklin,* ed. Leonard W. Labaree et al. (New Haven: Yale University Press, 1964), p. 43.

Autobiography) he leaves us with no doubt that his target is the Franklinian point of view.

Franklin's centrality, then, was found in this—that he seemed to incarnate the secularization of American ideals and to have deliberately fostered this outlook in his writing. Yet when Emerson and Thoreau protested, they were no more able than he to escape the individualistic drive in American life. Like him they possessed no coherent social theory, and in the Gilded Age Emerson's voice, with a show of plausibility, would actually be assimilated to Franklin's.[2] For

> Emerson...held a vision of the good society which had at its center the atomic individual, moving freely and without constraint through space and society, dependent upon nothing beyond his own personality and unaided self.[3]

American fiction, however, rejected the psychology of the unitary self and developed a searching critique of the social and political order that celebrated it. Exploring in concrete terms the actual needs of inner human nature and the relation of self to other, the fiction writers located in Franklin's thought and precipitated out of it for all to see a proclivity for the external and a cheapening of significance.

> I began now gradually to pay off the Debt I was under for the Printing-House. In order to secure my Credit and Character as a Tradesman, I took care not only to be in *Reality* Industrious and frugal, but to avoid all *Appearances* of the Contrary. I drest plainly; I was seen at no Places of idle Diversion; I never went out a-fishing or shooting; a Book, indeed, sometimes debauch'd me from my Work; but that was seldom, snug, and gave no Scandal: and to show that I was not above my Business, I sometimes brought home the Paper I purchas'd at the Stores, thro' the Streets on a Wheelbarrow. Thus being esteem'd an industrious thriving young Man, and paying duly for what I bought, the Merchants who imported Stationary solicited my Custom, others propos'd supplying me with Books, and I went on swimmingly.[4]

[2]Henry Bamford Parkes, *The American Experience* (New York: Vintage Books, 1959), pp. 265-66.

[3]John William Ward, "Individualism: Ideology or Utopia?" *Hastings Center Studies*, 2 (September 1974), 12.

[4]*Autobiography*, pp. 125-26.

Franklin is often accused of hypocrisy, but that is a much too superficial response to such passages as this. What ultimately seems to be involved is an implicit forswearing of the need to know life in its depths and, in the long run, a denial that such depths exist. This attitude has radical consequences for our ability to evaluate experience. Anyone who comes to the *Autobiography* fresh from Jonathan Edward's *Personal Narrative* (or the great and unfortunately neglected *Autobiography* of Thomas Shepard) recognizes that he has come into a world that, for all its sunlight, lacks perspective. There is no longer a third dimension, an order of reality beyond appearances. In Franklin's world the social, public reality is the only reality and the inner self is of no concern: man is what he is perceived to be by his society. And yet, at the same time, as with Emerson and Thoreau, there is no adequate sense of society in his work; it is only the sum of those atomistic individuals of which his own "I" is one.

This paradoxical definition of man—as a creature socially defined by what appears to be, and yet radically isolated in a society that is itself a matter of appearances—was a shaping pressure on *The Scarlet Letter.* Though Hawthorne set his novel in the Puritan past, it is at least as much a criticism of his American present, for the terrible isolation imposed by the Puritans upon Hester and Arthur in the face of their profound human need for community is expressive of contemporary social conditions. The Puritans are satisfied that their understanding of the case is adequate to its reality, that they have taken its measure. The allegorical "A" on Hester's breast is both the emblem of their understanding and the supposed means of her spiritual reconciliation. But the "A" that Hester wears is for Arthur, expressing a symbolic truth, like the labyrinth in which Hawthorne shows her wandering lost; the Puritans (good men, Hawthorne insists) look, pass on, perhaps smile, but do not see beyond surfaces. They cannot grasp the significance of what is before them, for a society of surfaces cannot fathom the symbolic signals of its members. Hawthorne's ironies, in showing the complexity of moral reality (enforced by the mesh imagery) and the difficulty of making contact with the depths of individual character, are an indictment of not only the Puritan society of Hester and Arthur, but also his own Franklinian society of surfaces.

The ability to grasp significance results from disciplined

cultivation of qualities of spirit, character, and mind, whereby a deepening sense of life comes to fuller consciousness. The Franklinian outlook, on the other hand, seemed to American writers to encourage an undiscerning satisfaction with the external and unfulfilling. Cooper sharply criticizes the commercial spirit, utilitarian habits of mind, and the cult of "general happy Mediocrity"[5] as a betrayal of the human meaning of the American experiment.[6] Poe's finest stories show, equally, how a prevailing emphasis on will and the orientation of life toward practical understanding can be seriously crippling.[7] Melville's *Bartleby* speaks to the same theme in reasserting, like *The Scarlet Letter,* a tragic view of life. In the first part the narrator (defined by his Franklinian characteristics—prudence, method, reasonableness) is governed by pity for Bartleby, in the second part by fear of him. But he is unable to coordinate these emotions or hold them in the single deepening focus of tragic experience. Though like Hawthorne's Puritan leaders he is a good and decent man moved by a certain degree of Christian charity, this only serves to sharpen the edge of Melville's criticism of a view of life without depth.

So fundamental is the criticism of Franklinian assumptions carved out by the greatest American writers of the nineteenth century that in the twentieth novelists like Fitzgerald and Faulkner found it obviously *there* to exploit. I have shown elsewhere how in *The Great Gatsby* Fitzgerald distinguishes the Emersonian and Franklinian dreams of America and identifies the Buchanans with the least attractive features of the Franklinian outlook.[8] In *Absalom, Absalom!,* too, Thomas Sutpen, with his utilitarian rationalism and imperviousness to both human personality and spiritual reality, his schedule, his design, his storybook rise to wealth, his desire to correct his mistake (his erratum?), embodies

---

[5]"Information to Those Who Would Remove to America," *The Writings of Benjamin Franklin,* ed. Albert Henry Smyth, 10 vols. (New York, 1907), 8: 604.

[6]Marius Bewley, *The Eccentric Design: Form in the Classic American Novel* (New York: Columbia University Press, 1957), pp. 22-100; Kay Seymour House, *Cooper's Americans* (Columbus: Ohio State University Press, 1965), pp. 117-46, 170.

[7]Brian M. Barbour, "Poe and Tradition," *Southern Literary Journal,* 10 (Spring 1978), 46-74.

[8]"*The Great Gatsby* and the American Past," *Southern Review,* 9 (Spring 1973), 288-99.

Franklinian characteristics and the Franklinian conception of success.

Thus Lawrence's essay was neither gratuitous nor, except in form, unprecedented. It was a response within an established tradition. There is after all a deeply ingrained tendency in American life that becomes most clearly explicable when related to Franklin, even though the historical Franklin was, of course, much greater than what was made of him. No one who examines his public career can feel anything but respect, and no one acquainted with American history can accuse him of having created the collection of attitudes that I have referred to here as the Franklinian outlook. He did, however, give these attitudes classic expression and thus a certain inner coherence, and he did—irresponsibly, I think—lend them his prestige, thus providing a moral endorsement. In any case, whatever his personal responsibility, a view of life strikingly compatible with the view taken in his autobiography came to dominate American society, and became for American writers infinitely repugnant, requiring of them, for their very morale as creators, the forging of a continuous critique. Franklin, therefore, is indispensable for the student of American literature and American civilization. Without understanding Franklin one cannot understand what followed.

II

Though modern scholars have tended to ignore the relationship of Lawrence's essay to tradition, they have not ignored the essay itself. Broadly speaking, three ways of defending Franklin have emerged. The first of these can be seen in the work of Carl Van Doren, who by a series of extravagant comparisons effectively put Franklin beyond the reach of negative judgment, but also beyond critical discussion.[9] The second is manifested in the work of Charles Sanford and Theodore Hornberger. These scholars

[9]See "Meet Dr. Franklin" and "Concluding Paper," both reprinted in *Benjamin Franklin and the American Character,* Charles L. Sanford, ed., (Boston: D.C. Heath, 1955), pp. 26-32, 93-98. The comparisons are to Leonardo da Vinci and Fielding: "If Franklin had put his mind to it he could have written as good novels as Fielding" (p. 94). It is only fair to add that in his biography Van Doren was more measured and that his services to Franklin scholarship were immense.

admit the general correctness of Lawrence's essay, but Sanford argues that Franklinianism actually reflects an "American sense of mission and a faith in moral regeneration based on a poetic conception of the frontier,"[10] while Hornberger chooses to emphasize Franklin's many other, less disputable achievements.[11] The third form of apologia is seen at its most distinguished in the essays by John William Ward and David Levin included here. They draw attention to the distinction between the historical Franklin who wrote the *Autobiography* and the character he portrays in it, giving us a fuller Franklin who is an intentional ironist and conscious literary craftsman. Out of this has come a body of scholarship engaged in study of Franklin's techniques, with special emphasis on his means of ordering his experience. This of course bears on Franklin's theme.

III

In this collection I have sought to bring together the best modern criticism on Franklin as a writer and moralist, though lack of space has prevented my including the paper by John Griffith listed in the bibliography. It will be seen at once that there is no unanimity of views among current critics but instead sharp disagreements that take the reader into central questions about American culture. The arrangement is meant to reflect the centrality of Lawrence's essay.

The first two pieces have a certain classical status. Becker argues that curiosity was Franklin's foremost trait and that this was fully aroused only in his scientific work, a view that tends quietly to confirm Lawrence's diagnosis. Weber adds that Poor Richard incarnated the spirit of capitalism as it emerged out of the Protestant ethic. Perry Miller points to the opposition of Franklin and Edwards as exemplifying a fundamental division in the American experience. Lewis P. Simpson's article comes from a group of pieces in which he maintains that in the eighteenth century there arose an order of secular men of letters indepen-

[10]Sanford, "An American *Pilgrim's Progress," American Quarterly,* 6 (Winter 1955), 297-310; reprinted in *Benjamin Franklin and the American Character,* pp. 64-73. The quote is from p. vii of the Introduction.

[11]Hornberger, *Benjamin Franklin,* University of Minnesota Pamphlets on American Writers (Minneapolis, 1962).

dent of church or state, whose Great Critique of feudal society opened the way for the mind's assumption of dominion and power. Printing was the means whereby the mind extended its realm, and the Declaration of Independence was the document that signaled the mind's new sovereignty. Franklin was the one great colonial philosophe to have had his hand in both. Daniel Shea examines the *Autobiography* against the tradition of spiritual autobiography and shows how completely Franklin has departed from it. After considering some features of Franklin's artistry he assesses the rival arguments of Lawrence and the ironists and makes the interesting suggestion (vigorously pursued in the succeeding chapter in his book) that Thoreau, Whitman, Dickinson, and Henry Adams all stand closer than Franklin to *spiritual* autobiography. Michael Gilmore is in Lawrence's tradition. What I have called a Franklinian outlook, he calls a secularized American ideology. His close scrutiny of the *Autobiography* leads him to the conviction that Franklin strove to defeat the religious past in order to foster economic individualism, his cardinal virtue. Franklin knew early what he wanted in prose, a style that was *"smooth, clear,* and *short."*[12] Since his gifts were for humor, homespun imagery, and the didactic, his greatest literary strengths lay in burlesque, comic instruction, and satire. The next three essays examine his comic techniques, and Professor Lemay shows how this comic skill could be effectively put in the service of Revolutionary politics. The final essay, by Louis B. Wright, demonstrates an important line of continuity between Franklin and the age of the Robber Barons.

Most of the essays here treat Franklin as a representative figure and, with the obvious exceptions, all deal with the *Autobiography.* Few other Americans seem, in Perry Miller's words, so "massively symbolic," and no other book, Emerson's essays not excepted, has had so profound, so nearly irresistible an influence on our civilization.

[12]"On Literary Style," *The Papers of Benjamin Franklin,* ed. Leonard W. Labaree et al., 20 vols. to date (New Haven: Yale University Press, 1959-), 1: 329.

Franklin's Character

by Carl L. Becker

Great men are often hampered by some inner discord or want of harmony with the world in which they live. It was Franklin's good fortune to have been endowed with a rare combination of rare qualities, and to have lived at a time when circumstances favored the development of all his powers to their fullest extent. He was a true child of the Enlightenment, not indeed of the school of Rousseau, but of Defoe and Pope and Swift, of Fontenelle and Montesquieu and Voltaire. He spoke their language, although with a homely accent, a tang of the soil, that bears witness to his lowly and provincial origin. His wit and humor, lacking indeed the cool, quivering brilliance of Voltaire or the corrosive bitterness of Pope and Swift, were all the more effective and humane for their dash of genial and kindly cynicism. He accepted without question and expressed without effort all the characteristic ideas and prepossessions of the century—its aversion to "superstition" and "enthusiasms" and mystery; its contempt for hocus-pocus and its dislike of dim perspectives; its healthy, clarifying scepticism; its passion for freedom and its humane sympathies; its preoccupation with the world that is evident to the senses; its profound faith in common sense, in the efficacy of Reason for the solution of human problems and the advancement of human welfare.

For impressing his age with the validity of these ideas, both by precept and example, Franklin's native qualities were admirably suited. His mind, essentially pragmatic and realistic, by pref-

"Franklin's Character." Adaptation of Carl Becker's article "Benjamin Franklin" reprinted from *The Dictionary of American Biography* with the permission of Charles Scribner's Sons. Copyright © 1930, 1931, American Council of Learned Societies. This is the conclusion of the article.

erence occupied itself with what was before it, with the present
rather than with the past or the future, with the best of possible
rather than with the best of conceivable worlds. He accepted men
and things, including himself, as they were, with a grain of salt
indeed but with insatiable curiosity, with irrepressible zest and
good humor. He took life as it came, with the full-blooded hearti-
ness of a man unacquainted with inhibitions and repressions and
spiritual *malaise,* as a game to be played, with honesty and sincerity, but with shrewdness and an eye to the main chance, above
all without pontifical solemnity, without self-pity, eschewing vain
regrets for lost illusions and vain striving for the light that never
was. Both his achievements and his limitations spring from this:
that he accepted the world as given with imperturbable serenity;
without repining identified himself with it; and brought to the
understanding and mastery of it rare common sense, genuine
disinterestedness, a fertile and imaginative curiosity, and a cool,
flexible intelligence fortified by exact knowledge and chastened
and humanized by practical activities.

Not only was Franklin by temperament disposed to take life as
it came and to make the most of it; in addition fate provided him
with a rich diversity of experience such as has rarely fallen to the
lot of any man. Rising from poverty to affluence, from obscurity
to fame, he lived on every social level in turn, was equally at ease
with rich and poor, the cultivated and the untutored, and spoke
with equal facility the language of vagabonds and kings, politi-
cians and philosophers, men of letters, kitchen girls, and *femmes
savantes.* Reared in Boston, a citizen of Philadelphia, residing for
sixteen years in London and for nine in Paris, he was equally at
home in three countries, knew Europe better than any other
American, America better than any European, England better
than most Frenchmen, France better than most Englishmen, and
was acquainted personally or through correspondence with more
men of eminence in letters, science, and politics than any other
man of his time. Such a variety of experience would have confused and disoriented any man less happily endowed with a capacity for assimilating it. Franklin took it all easily, relishing it,
savoring it, without rest and without haste adding to his knowledge, fortifying and tempering his intelligence, broadening his
point of view, humanizing and mellowing his tolerant acceptance

of men and things—in short chastening and perfecting the qualities that were natively his; so that in the end he emerges the most universal and cosmopolitan spirit of his age. Far more a "good European," a citizen of the world, than Adams or Jefferson, Washington or Hutchinson, he remained to the end more pungently American than any of them. Jefferson said that Franklin was the one exception to the rule that seven years of diplomatic service abroad spoiled an American. Twenty-five years of almost continuous residence abroad did not spoil Franklin. Acclaimed and decorated as no American had ever been, he returned to Philadelphia and was immediately at home again, easily recognizable by his neighbors as the man they had always known—Ben Franklin, printer.

The secret of Franklin's amazing capacity for assimilating experience without being warped or discolored by it is perhaps to be found in his disposition to take life with infinite zest and yet with humorous detachment. Always immersed in affairs, he seems never completely absorbed by them; mastering easily whatever comes his way, there remain powers in reserve never wholly engaged. It is significant that his activities, with the exception of his researches in science, seem to have been the result, not of any compelling inner impulse or settled purpose, but rather of the pressure of external need or circumstance. He was a business man, and a good one; but having won a competence he retired. He was an inventor and a philanthropist, but not by profession; perceiving the need, he invented a stove or founded a hospital. He was a politician and a diplomat, and none more skilled; but not from choice; for the most part he accepted as a duty the offices that were thrust upon him. He was a writer, a prolific one; yet his writings were nearly all occasional, prompted by the need of the moment. His one book, the *Autobiography*, was begun as something that might be useful to his son; that purpose served, it was never finished. He was a literary artist of rare merit, the master of a style which for clarity, precision, and pliable adhesion to the form and pressure of the idea to be conveyed has rarely been equalled. Yet once having learned the trade he was little preoccupied with the art of writing, content to throw off in passing an acute pragmatic definition: Good writing "ought to have a tendency to benefit the reader. ... But taking the question otherwise, an ill man may write an ill thing well. ... In this sense, that is well wrote, which is best adapted for obtaining the end of the writer."[1] It has been said that Franklin was not entrusted with the task of writing the Declaration of Independence for fear he might conceal a joke in the middle of it. The myth holds a profound symbolic truth. In all of Franklin's dealings with men and affairs, genuine, sincere, loyal as he surely was, one feels that he is nevertheless not wholly committed; some thought remains uncommunicated; some penetrating observation is held in reserve. In spite of his ready attention to the business in hand, there is something casual about his efficient dispatch of it; he manages somehow to remain aloof, a spectator still, with amiable curiosity watching himself functioning effectively in the world. After all men were but children needing to be cajoled; affairs a game not to be played without finesse. Was there not then, on that placid countenance, even at the signing of the great Declaration, the bland smile which seems to say: This is an interesting, alas even a necessary, game; and we are playing it well, according to all the rules; but men being what they are it is perhaps best not to inquire too curiously what its ultimate significance may be.

One exception there was—science: one activity which Franklin pursued without outward prompting, from some compelling inner impulse; one activity from which he never wished to retire, to which he would willingly have devoted his life, to which he always gladly turned in every odd day or hour of leisure, even in the midst of the exacting duties and heavy responsibilities of his public career. Science was after all the one mistress to whom he gave himself without reserve and served neither from a sense of duty nor for any practical purpose. Nature alone met him on equal terms, with a disinterestedness matching his own; needing not to be cajoled or managed with finesse, she enlisted in the solution of her problems the full power of his mind. In dealing with nature he could be, as he could not be in dealing with men and affairs, entirely sincere, pacific, objective, rational, could speak his whole thought without reservation, with no suggestion of a stupendous cosmic joke concealed in the premises. Franklin was indeed "many-sided." From the varied facets of his powerful mind he threw a brilliant light on all aspects of human life; it is

[1] *The Writings of Benjamin Franklin,* ed. Albert H. Smyth (New York: Macmillan, 1905-07), I: 37.

only in his character of natural philosopher that he emits a light quite unclouded. It is in this character therefore that the essential quality of the man appears to best advantage. Sir Humphry Davy has happily noted it for us.

> The experiments adduced by Dr. Franklin...were most ingeniously contrived and happily executed. A singular felicity of induction guided all his researches, and by very small means he established very grand truths. The style and manner of his publication [on electricity] are almost as worthy of admiration as the doctrine it contains. He has endeavored to remove all mystery and obscurity from the subject; he has written equally for the uninitiated and for the philosopher; and he has rendered his details amusing as well as perspicuous, elegant as well as simple. Science appears in his language in a dress wonderfully decorous, the best adapted to display her native loveliness. He has in no case exhibited that false dignity, by which philosophy is kept aloof from common applications, and he has sought rather to make her a useful inmate and servant in the common habitations of man, than to preserve her merely as an object of admiration in temples and palaces.[2]

[2]*The collected Works of Sir Humphry Davy* (London, 1839-40), VIII: 264-65.

The Spirit of Capitalism

by Max Weber

In the title of this study is used the somewhat pretentious phrase, the *spirit* of capitalism. What is to be understood by it? The attempt to give anything like a definition of it brings out certain difficulties which are in the very nature of this type of investigation.

If any object can be found to which this term can be applied with any understandable meaning, it can only be an historical individual, i.e. a complex of elements associated in historical reality which we unite into a conceptual whole from the standpoint of their cultural significance.

Such an historical concept, however, since it refers in its content to a phenomenon significant for its unique individuality, cannot be defined according to the formula *genus proximum, differentia specifica,* but it must be gradually put together out of the individual parts which are taken from historical reality to make it up. Thus the final and definitive concept cannot stand at the beginning of the investigation, but must come at the end. We must, in other words, work out in the course of the discussion, as its most important result, the best conceptual formulation of what we here understand by the spirit of capitalism, that is the best from the point of view which interests us here. This point of view (the one of which we shall speak later) is, further, by no means the only possible one from which the historical phenomena we are investigating can be analysed. Other standpoints would, for this as for every historical phenomenon, yield other characteristics as the essential ones. The result is that it is by no means necessary to understand by the spirit of capitalism only what it will come to mean to *us* for the purposes of our analysis. This is a necessary result of the nature of historical concepts which attempt for their methodological purposes not to grasp historical reality in abstract general formulae, but in concrete genetic sets of relations which are inevitably of a specifically unique and individual character.

Thus, if we try to determine the object, the analysis and historical explanation of which we are attempting, it cannot be in the form of a conceptual definition, but at least in the beginning only a provisional description of what is here meant by the spirit of capitalism. Such a description is, however, indispensable in order clearly to understand the object of the investigation. For this purpose we turn to a document of that spirit which contains what we are looking for in almost classical purity, and at the same time has the advantage of being free from all direct relationship to religion, being thus, for our purposes, free of preconceptions.

> Remember, that *time* is money. He that can earn ten shillings a day by his labour, and goes abroad, or sits idle, one half of that day, though he spends but sixpence during his diversion or idleness, ought not to reckon *that* the only expense; he has really spent, or rather thrown away, five shillings besides.
>
> Remember, that *credit* is money. If a man lets his money lie in my hands after it is due, he gives me the interest, or so much as I can make of it during that time. This amounts to a considerable sum where a man has good and large credit, and makes good use of it.
>
> Remember, that money is of the prolific, generating nature. Money can beget money, and its offspring can beget more, and so on. Five shillings turned is six, turned again it is seven and three-pence, and so on, till it becomes a hundred pounds. The more there is of it, the more it produces every turning, so that the profits rise quicker and quicker. He that kills a breeding-sow, destroys all her offspring to the thousandth generation. He that murders a crown, destroys all that it might have produced, even scores of pounds.
>
> Remember this saying, *The good paymaster is lord of another man's purse.* He that is known to pay punctually and exactly to the time he promises, may at any time, and on any occasion, raise all the money his friends can spare. This is sometimes of great use. After industry and frugality, nothing contributes more to the raising of a young man in the world than punctuality and justice in

all his dealings; therefore never keep borrowed money an hour beyond the time you promised, lest a disappointment shut up your friend's purse forever.

The most trifling actions that affect a man's credit are to be regarded. The sound of your hammer at five in the morning, or eight at night, heard by a creditor, makes him easy six months longer; but if he sees you at a billiard-table, or hears your voice at a tavern, when you should be at work, he sends for his money the next day; demands it, before he can receive it, in a lump.

It shows, besides, that you are mindful of what you owe; it makes you appear a careful as well as an honest man, and that still increases your credit.

Beware of thinking all your own that you possess, and of living accordingly. It is a mistake that many people who have credit fall into. To prevent this, keep an exact account for some time both of your expenses and your income. If you take the pains at first to mention particulars, it will have this good effect: you will discover how wonderfully small, trifling expenses mount up to large sums, and will discern what might have been, and may for the future be saved, without occasioning any great inconvenience.

For six pounds a year you may have the use of one hundred pounds, provided you are a man of known prudence and honesty.

He that spends a groat a day idly, spends idly above six pounds a year, which is the price for the use of one hundred pounds.

He that wastes idly a groat's worth of his time per day, one day with another, wastes the privilege of using one hundred pounds each day.

He that idly loses five shillings worth of time, loses five shillings, and might as prudently throw five shillings into the sea.

He that loses five shillings, not only loses that sum, but all the advantage that might be made by turning it in dealing, which by the time that a young man becomes old, will amount to a considerable sum of money.[1]

It is Benjamin Franklin who preaches to us in these sentences, the same which Ferdinand Kürnberger satirizes in his clever and malicious *Picture of American Culture* as the supposed confession of faith of the Yankee. That it is the spirit of capitalism which here speaks in characteristic fashion, no one will doubt,

[1]The final passage is from "Necessary Hints to Those That Would Be Rich" (written 1736), *The Works of Benjamin Franklin*, ed. Jared Sparks (Boston, 1836-40), II: 80; the rest is from "Advice to a Young Tradesman" (written 1748), *Works*, II: 87 ff. Italics in the text are Franklin's.

however little we may wish to claim that everything which could be understood as pertaining to that spirit is contained in it. Let us pause a moment to consider this passage, the philosophy of which Kürnberger sums up in the words, "They make tallow out of cattle and money out of men." The peculiarity of this philosophy of avarice appears to be the ideal of the honest man of recognized credit, and above all the idea of a duty of the individual toward the increase of his capital, which is assumed as an end in itself. Truly what is here preached is not simply a means of making one's way in the world, but a peculiar ethic. The infraction of its rules is treated not as foolishness but as forgetfulness of duty. That is the essence of the matter. It is not mere business astuteness, that sort of thing is common enough, it is an ethos. *This* is the quality which interests us.

When Jacob Fugger, in speaking to a business associate who had retired and who wanted to persuade him to do the same, since he had made enough money and should let others have a chance, rejected that as pusillanimity and answered that "he (Fugger) thought otherwise, he wanted to make money as long as he could," the spirit of his statement is evidently quite different from that of Franklin. What in the former case was an expression of commercial daring and a personal inclination morally neutral,[2] in the latter takes on the character of an ethically coloured maxim for the conduct of life. The concept spirit of capitalism is here used in this specific sense, it is the spirit of modern capitalism. For that we are here dealing only with Western European and American capitalism is obvious from the way in which the problem was stated. Capitalism existed in China, India, Babylon, in the classic world, and in the Middle Ages. But in all these cases, as we shall see, this particular ethos was lacking.

Now, all Franklin's moral attitudes are coloured with utilitarianism. Honesty is useful, because it assures credit; so are

[2]Which quite obviously does not mean either that Jacob Fugger was a morally indifferent or an irreligious man, or that Benjamin Franklin's ethic is completely covered by the above quotations. It scarcely required Lujo Brentano's quotations *(Die Anfange des modernen Kapitalismus* [Munich, 1916] , pp. 150 ff.) to protect this well-known philanthropist from the misunderstanding which Brentano seems to attribute to me. The problem is just the reverse: how could such a philanthropist come to write these particular sentences (the especially characteristic form of which Brentano has neglected to reproduce) in the manner of a moralist?

punctuality, industry, frugality, and that is the reason they are virtues. A logical deduction from this would be that where, for instance, the appearance of honesty serves the same purpose, that would suffice, and an unnecessary surplus of this virtue would evidently appear to Franklin's eyes as unproductive waste. And as a matter of fact, the story in his autobiography of his conversion to those virtues,[3] or the discussion of the value of a strict maintenance of the appearance of modesty, the assiduous belittlement of one's own deserts in order to gain general recognition later,[4] confirms this impression. According to Franklin, those virtues, like all others, are only in so far virtues as they are actually useful to the individual, and the surrogate of mere appearance is always sufficient when it accomplishes the end in view. It is a conclusion which is inevitable for strict utilitarianism. The impression of many Germans that the virtues professed by Americanism are pure hypocrisy seems to have been confirmed by this striking case. But in fact the matter is not by any means so simple. Benjamin Franklin's own character, as it appears in the really unusual candidness of his autobiography, belies that suspicion. The circumstance that he ascribes his recognition of the utility of virtue to a divine revelation which was intended to lead him in the path of righteousness, shows that something more than mere garnishing for purely egocentric motives is involved.

[3]"I grew convinced that truth, sincerity, and integrity in dealings between man and man were of the utmost importance to the felicity of life; and I formed written resolutions, which still remain in my journal book, to practice them ever while I lived. Revelation had indeed no weight with me as such; but I entertained an opinion that, though certain actions might not be bad because they were forbidden by it, or good because it commanded them, yet probably these actions might be forbidden because they were bad for us, or commanded because they were beneficial to us in their own nature, all the circumstances of things considered." *Autobiography*, ed. F. W. Pine (New York: Henry Holt, 1916), p. 112.

[4]"I therefore put myself as much as I could out of sight and started it" — that is, the project of a library which he had initiated — "as a scheme of a *number of friends,* who had requested me to go about and propose it to such as they thought lovers of reading. In this way my affair went on smoothly, and I ever after practiced it on such occasions; and from my frequent successes, can heartily recommend it. The present little sacrifice of your vanity will afterwards be amply repaid. If it remains awhile uncertain to whom the merit belongs, someone more vain than yourself will be encouraged to claim it, and then even envy will be disposed to do you justice by plucking those assumed feathers and restoring them to their right owner." *The Autobiography of Benjamin Franklin,* p. 140.

In fact, the *summum bonum* of this ethic, the earning of more and more money, combined with the strict avoidance of all spontaneous enjoyment of life, is above all completely devoid of any eudemonistic, not to say hedonistic, admixture. It is thought of so purely as an end in itself, that from the point of view of the happiness of, or utility to, the single individual, it appears entirely transcendental and absolutely irrational. Man is dominated by the making of money, by acquisition as the ultimate purpose of his life. Economic acquisition is no longer subordinated to man as the means for satisfaction of his material needs. This reversal of what we should call the natural relationship, so irrational from a naive point of view, is evidently as definitely a leading principle of capitalism as it is foreign to all peoples not under capitalistic influence. At the same time it expresses a type of feeling which is closely connected with certain religious ideas. If we thus ask, *why* should "money be made out of men," Benjamin Franklin himself, although he was a colourless deist, answers in his autobiography with a quotation from the Bible, which his strict Calvinistic father drummed into him again and again in his youth: "Seest thou a man diligent in his business? He shall stand before kings" (Proverbs, xxii, 29). The earning of money within the modern economic order is, so long as it is done legally, the result and the expression of virtue and proficiency in a calling; and this virtue and proficiency are, as it is now not difficult to see, the real Alpha and Omega of Franklin's ethic, as expressed in the passages we have quoted, as well as in all his works without exception.

Franklin and the Divided Heritage of Puritanism

by Perry Miller

The intellectual history—or, if you will, the spiritual history—of the United States has been dramatized by a series of pairs of personalities, contemporaneous and contrasting, which have become avatars of the contradictory thrusts within our effort to find or to create a national identity.

To begin with, there is in primordial Virginia a swashbuckling adventurer, Captain John Smith, frankly announcing that only the search for wealth will found a commonwealth and that the wilderness will become a theater of gigantic economic exploitation; whereas, on the rock-bound and unfertile coast of New England there is William Bradford directing an energy no less Elizabethan toward the realization of a holy society. After the Revolution emerge the exemplary figures of Jefferson and Hamilton, who form the division between the political convictions that have since contended for mastery. In the Civil War the sectional strife finds its perfect symbolism in the opposition of Robert E. Lee and Abraham Lincoln. But of all these, and of several lesser pairs, the pre-eminently eloquent linked antagonists in American culture will always be Jonathan Edwards and Benjamin Franklin.

This duel is all the more eloquent, not because the two met in open debate, as did Jefferson and Hamilton in the 1790's—they showed little or no awareness of each other's existence—but because they started in their contrary directions from the same parent stock, the Puritanism of New England. Each may be said to realize a potentiality that in the original creed was concealed beneath the supposed unity of this highly systematized version of Protestantism. As they divide the heritage between them, Franklin and Edwards expose the inner tensions which not only the Puritans but all Protestant immigrants—the Dutch and Scotch-Irish Presbyterians, Baptists, Quakers, German Calvinists and Lutherans, and eventually the Methodists—brought to these shores. They make wonderfully clear how this incipient civil war within the piety could be brought into the open only by the conditions of this new world, where there were not the social or institutional complexities which in Europe prevented it from preempting the center of the intellectual stage.

Puritans originally got their name from their enemies, because their avowed purpose in England was to "purify" the Church of England from what they considered the remnants of medieval Catholicism that still adhered to it—the hierarchy, vestments, prescribed prayers, and stated forms of traditional ritual. They declared that the Church should be stripped of these "rags and tatters of the Whore of Babylon"—to use their blunt language—until it was reduced to the sparse simplicity of organization and conduct which they believed had been meticulously set forth in the New Testament. Hence the Churchmen called them "Puritans," but also, in still angrier derision, more exactly, "Precisians." Puritans wanted life to be regulated precisely by the rules of the supreme legal code of Christendom, the whole Bible, which in their comprehension provided precepts for all departments of life—for family, economic activity, and political policy as well as for ecclesiastical polity. In theology the Puritans were at one with the other branches of international Calvinism—Swiss, French, German, Dutch, and Scottish. But in this vast communion, the English Puritans were distinguished by the zeal with which they pressed theological considerations into the secular realms of human behavior.

A few of them, generally of the simpler and less prosperous sort, were so impelled by this temper that they became, as Bradford recounts, "Separatists." Wherefore, they were harried out of the land. One band eventually became the Pilgrims of Plymouth in Massachusetts Bay. However, the majority of Puritans refused to "separate" because they wanted to fight within the Church for

ultimate conquest. They did not want even toleration, let alone
liberty: they intended to rule. In 1630 that hope had become
remote; hence a compact company, having somehow secured a
charter from Charles I which bestowed legality upon the venture,
arrived at the site of Boston. In the next decade some ten thousand followed; these expanded across Massachusetts and into
Connecticut; from them comes everything that has been praised
or cursed in America under the name of "Puritanism." From their
ranks come the two most distinguished intellects and prose
artists of the tradition, who in these selections pose for us the
paradox of Puritan materialism and immateriality.

The inmost essence of the Puritan spirit is certainly embodied
in the cadences of William Bradford. Yet, since he was a Separa-
tist, he is not quite representative of the mass of Puritan immigrants to New England. Edward Taylor, in his isolation at
Westfield, was driven to an inward analysis of his spiritual condition which is the heart of the Puritan's demand upon himself—
that nervous tic of introspection which survives even today as
what has been nicknamed, generally in tones of ridicule, "The
New England Conscience." Still, in his secret self-examinations
through verses of a "metaphysical" sort, he was also unrepre-
sentative of the dominant literary ethos. In the New England of
Taylor's time, and in the youthful decades of both Edwards and
Franklin, this rule was deliberately termed the "plaine stile."
Both Edwards and Franklin are thus heirs of a once unitary tradition, which they split asunder but of which they are alike
legitimate descendants. Franklin in the life of the world and
Edwards in the life of the spirit both strove for, and each in his
widely differing manner attained, a clarity, simplicity, directness
—a suppression of all showy and "literary" embellishments—
which is the lasting impress of the Puritan spirit upon American
expression. Not, of course, that many writers have not revolted
against it, including several lineal descendants of the Puritan
founders; but on the whole, one is safe in saying, the literature of
America is marked by its concern, often neurotic rather than
sanative, that literature be not regarded as an end in itself, but
that expression be put to work in the service of a creed, a career,
a philosophy, a disgruntlement or a rage.

This rule of efficiency as the governing purpose of the spoken or written word was part and parcel of the conception Puritans brought into the control of all areas of their behavior, most strenuously into that of their pecuniary labor. The whole complex of that code has been summarized by modern sociologists as "the Protestant ethic." Though elements of it may be found in all the emerging business cultures of the time, the English Puritans perfected it more highly than others in Europe, and the New England Puritans brought it to an even higher degree of articulation. Edwards in his pulpit and in his study, Franklin in his printing shop and in the diplomatic chambers of Versailles were both assiduously practicing the ethic of their fathers.

Fundamentally, this mentality was a revulsion against what Protestants held to be the unprofitable monasticism of the Medieval Church, which centered holiness upon withdrawal from the economy of production and distribution, which consigned these crass functions to the inferior orders of peasants or merchants. Instead, the Puritans declared, every "calling"—whether it be ditch-digging, fishing, sailing a vessel, managing a bank, governing a colony or preaching a sermon—was as much a religious exercise as any other. In this view the clergy, though of course commissioned to instruct the yeomen in faith and morals, were no whit superior to their pupils. The great sin in their society was to endeavor to live without a calling, without being industrious at *something,* as did both the Catholic monk and the European nobleman. The Rev. John Cotton, in the classic New England formulation (printed in 1641, but spoken earlier), said, "If thou beest a man that lives without a calling, though thou has two thousands to spend, yet if thou hast no calling tending to public good, thou art an unclean beast." Yet the ethic was more subtle than merely an injunction to find a job and to work in it as a holy duty: it insisted that energy expended in a calling be regarded as a service for God, and not as a means of profit or of social betterment. Wherefore the Puritan exerts himself the more vigorously in proportion to the more, again in the language of Cotton, "he depends upon God for the quickening and sharpening of his gifts in that calling." That is, he applies himself stoutly, but he attributes success not to his efforts but only to the favor, the complaisance, of God. Likewise, if despite his most energetic performance he encounters disaster—a shipwreck, a plague of locusts, a military defeat—he perceives in the reversal a chastisement of the Lord, rained upon him for his sins. Thereupon he renews with increased vigor his assault upon prosperity.

Therefore, let us be clear that for the Puritan founders the same rationale served in either ditch-digging or manufacturing as in the physical act of putting words on paper: nobody was doing it to amuse himself or others, and not directly with the intention of making money or winning converts. He was doing the job in obedience to the commands of God, or of conscience, or of probity; but he did not, if he was sanctified, bank upon his own talents for success. He cultivated and improved them assiduously, day and night, in order to make an acceptable sacrifice of them to the Puritan Jehovah, who might then be graciously inclined to bestow the desired results, but who might also be inclined, with every right on His side, to reward the desperate effort with complete devastation. Although Franklin blithely put aside the theology out of which this peculiar code arose, he as much as Edwards exemplified it every day of his life. And Edwards, even while refashioning the Jehovah of early Puritanism into a highly impersonalized design of the Newtonian universe, went on offering himself a willing victim to the whims of a Divinity bound by no such rules of justice as were supposed to prevail in human intercourse.

For Edwards, the endeavor resulted in ghastly failure, in the abject humiliation of his dismissal from the Northampton pulpit in 1750, and in his eight years of penurious exile in Stockbridge. For Franklin, the application produced wealth, fame, and the universal approbation of his contemporaries and of posterity. Both of them, in the center of their beings, were indifferent to the consequences, ill or bountiful; both were so caught up, with or without theology, in a vision of ultimate disinterestedness in relation to which either personal triumph or defeat was inconsequential, that the most ethereal writings of Edwards can be easily translated into the most mundane of Franklin's frivolities. Yet the division is not superficial: it is profound, irreconcilable. It also provides a theme, probably the basic and sundering theme, of American literature.

Franklin and Emerson

by Brian M. Barbour

...In *The Great Gatsby* Tom and Daisy Buchanan represent
a quality, a permanent tendency that runs all through American
life and which finds its source in Benjamin Franklin.

The Great Gatsby is about the American dream—so the truism
goes. But the truism in this case is too clumsy, for there are actually two American dreams and *The Great Gatsby* is about them both
and the way they interact. It is convenient to employ metonymy
and identify these two dreams with the two figures who first
articulated them and thereby brought them to consciousness:
Franklin and Ralph Waldo Emerson.

Franklin's dream is the dream of *freedom-from* that D. H.
Lawrence complained about so bitterly in *Studies in Classic
American Literature*. The *Autobiography* is a book shaped by
fear, the fear of arbitrary power—tyranny—that prevents a man
from becoming himself. The form this fear takes is economic.
What does Franklin teach us? That a man has to acquire a certain
amount of necessary wealth so that his destiny will be in his own
hands and not those of his creditors. Without wealth no man is
free—that is the book's secret motto. It is no use being superior
about this motto. Franklin was articulating something deep in
human consciousness and something given power by the intellectual and political currents of the time. America can be the land of
the free because in America every man can acquire the minimum
wealth necessary to be his own man. It's a dream not far different
from Jefferson's, and it was certainly never intended to license the
Robber Barons. But what we must pay attention to is its focus and

direction. It is a view that looks exclusively to the past and defines itself in relation to that past. In a way it is transfixed by that past to the extent that it never turns its face forward and asks itself where it is going and what its consequences are. It is so exclusively concerned with *getting free* that it has no energy left for exploring the meaning of its freedom. The wealth that bestows freedom validates itself. Vulgarized, what this means is that wealth is not just means but end; because it means freedom it need not be questioned by any standard beyond itself. (That the emergence of this idea happened to coincide with the vulgarization of certain aspects of Calvinist theology — the Puritan Ethic argument — was doubly unfortunate, for not only was a possible higher standard for judgment lost, but the new tendency received a firm moral — sometimes religious — endorsement.) Having become free, Franklinian man is spared the necessity of having to ask himself, What for? What is my freedom for?

Franklin himself did not entirely escape this vulgarization. It is present in the *Autobiography* in two distinct ways. The first and most famous of these is the schedule of virtues that is attached to the plan for moral perfection. All that needs to be said about them was said long ago by Lawrence. They are hopelessly trivial and the sense of life they betray is likewise trivial. The second is to be found in the basic structure of the book itself. The principle of organization is the anecdotal moral lesson. He retails little events from his past and then points out the lesson to be learned. Franklin was a skilled comic writer and his life gave him a fund of rich material, but because there is no deeper sense of life working through and organizing the material it becomes hopelessly repetitious and finally boring. One reads up to the famous plan and perhaps a little beyond, but the book is unreadable straight through and no one is likely to mind that it went unfinished.

The *Autobiography,* nevertheless, is the most influential book ever written by an American. It organized, expressed, and made eminently respectable a concept of human life that is seriously deficient but which does not know itself to be so. The view it expresses is the bourgeois outlook of Main Street, and its American dream has been casually and complacently erected into the implicit goal of American life. What makes it pernicious is that the value-words on which it depends, especially freedom, are invoked but not defined. In the nature of the case they cannot easily be, but there is present no reason for feeling that they *should* be. The Franklinian dream, then, is one of self-validating materialism that is ignorant about the inner, positive meaning of the freedom it posits as its end, and is in fact complacently blind with respect to any positive moral values or genuinely spiritual sense of human life. The Buchanans embody it in its least attractive form.

Emerson's role as an antipode to Franklin has never been adequately stressed, yet it is possible to say that his whole career was a quarrel with the Franklinian spirit and the Franklinian dream. "Quarrel" is perhaps inadequate to suggest that in every line he indited Emerson was warring against the Franklinian outlook. The main thrust of his career was an attempt to take the American dream away from the Franklinians ("the Party of Memory," he called them) and to redefine it in moral and spiritual terms. For Emerson, too, the meaning of America was associated with freedom, but he set out to explore the nature and consequence of that freedom and to determine its effect on human life. He too articulated an American dream, but one moral and spiritual and always in the state of becoming. It is not a little significant that when—as in *The American Scholar* and *Self-Reliance*—Emerson goes on the attack he writes against an attitude that he posits in unmistakable Franklinian imagery: the "iron lids" of the "sluggard intellect" that never rises above "mechanical skill" and so results in a spirit that is "timid, imitative, tame"; or "the reliance on Property" no matter if it comes through "gift, inheritance, or crime" that marks "the want of self-reliance."

Self-reliance is the foremost Franklinian virtue; it is also the title of Emerson's most powerful essay, and the fundamental differences between the two American dreams can be seen by comparing the inner meanings the concept had for the two men. For Franklin it is a reliance on one's self as an accumulator of wealth; that is, it is a means for becoming free from the power of another. It is indivisible from the credit-enhancing self-discipline which is the highest mark of character. Because this self-reliance *works*—i.e., because it does lead to wealth—the inevitable tendency is to over-value this self of the marketplace, to feel secure in its power and certain of its capacity. And this in turn leads to the moral complacency that abandons any rigorous scrutiny of means and ends and which does not feel itself to be called on to answer any of the deeper questions about life. Its self is a satisfied self. This is most easily seen in the pitch-note of optimism (or, at its most vulgar, backslapping, flank-rubbing geniality) which has always keyed the Franklinian dream and which is not an optimism that has taken the measure of things, but is only a lack of contact with or concern for any adequate concept of evil or with the tragic sense. Franklin rose above this through his ideal of public service. But often no such ideal exists, and after the status of leisure has been attained, there is no sense of what to do with it. Life flattens out into a string of "Tomorrow and tomorrow and tomorrow...." "'What'll we do with ourselves this afternoon?' cried Daisy, 'and the day after that, and the next thirty years?'"

For Emerson self-reliance was based on trust, but it was decidedly not a trust in the ordinary self of the marketplace. That self had to be redeemed. Self-reliance begins with a reliance on God and it moves through a purgation of the ordinary self. That movement is from the ordinary self existing at the level of Franklinian materialism to the new self that has left materialism behind in order to live in the spirit. "The one thing in the world, of value, is the active soul." The whole of Emerson's thought is contained in that one sentence with its startling reassessment of the concept of *value*. Where Franklin is concerned with being and having, Emerson is concerned with being and becoming. Where Franklin is concerned with accumulating energy, Emerson is concerned with releasing it. Where Franklin looks to the past to secure his definition and meaning, Emerson looks to the future. Freedom is the condition for man's exploration of the new, higher self. "This one fact the world hates: that the soul *becomes;* for that forever degrades the past, turns all riches to poverty, all respect to shame."

It is difficult to translate the Emersonian vision, with its strong overlaying of mysticism, into the language of ordinary discourse. At his greatest moments Emerson was operating at the frontiers of language, and he knew what obstacles that raised to communication. But it is enough to note the positive, idealist structure of the Emersonian dream, and to note too the stern standard of *character* which Emerson assumed. He had nothing to offer triflers. The real secret of the Emersonian self is that, in contradistinction to the Franklinian self based on wealth, it depends on the moral ground of its own bedrock puritanism. Much of its power lies in its promise to free the ordinary self from the materialism, stagnancy, and moral complacency of the enacted Franklinian dream. Its promise is in the future; it lies in becoming and poses the deepest of moral challenges. In attempting to articulate it, Emerson threw Franklin's dream into a new perspective. Once both are brought to consciousness, the moral deficiency and adolescent cast of Franklin's become glaring. One has to leave it behind and pursue the higher truth. Emerson was a true moral teacher: he called on men to change their lives. His vision involved nothing less than a fundamental revaluation of the meaning of the American experience. The new self is to be a moral self whose duty is to be always becoming, always extending and newly articulating the possibilities of life. "The truth was that Jay Gatsby...sprang from his Platonic conception of himself. He was a son of God. ..."

The Printer as a Man of Letters: Franklin and the Symbolism of the Third Realm

by Lewis P. Simpson

"I, Benjamin Franklin, of Philadelphia, printer, late Minister Plenipotentiary for the United States of America to the Court of France, and President of the State of Pennsylvania..."[1]

Although he had not followed the printing trade since 1748, when he had withdrawn from active participation in a printing and bookselling house to enter upon his various and widely influential public life as man of letters and statesman, Franklin recognized in his last will and testament in 1788 that the second part of his career was at one with the first. He confirmed the prophecy of his career made at the age of twenty-two, when the youthful Philadelphia printer, suffering from pleurisy, had somewhat prematurely composed his own epitaph.

The body of
B Franklin Printer
(Like the Cover of an old Book
Its Contents torn out
And stript of its Lettering & Gilding)
Lies here, Food for Worms.
But the Work shall not be lost;
For it will, (as he believ'd) appear once more,
In a new and more elegant Edition
Revised and corrected
By the Author.

"The Printer as a Man of Letters: Franklin and the Symbolism of the Third Realm." From *The Oldest Revolutionary: Essays on Benjamin Franklin*, ed. J.A. Leo Lemay. Copyright © 1976 by the University of Pennsylvania Press. Reprinted by permission of the publisher.

[1]Quoted in Carl Van Doren, *Benjamin Franklin* (New York: Garden City Publishing Company, 1941), p. 123.

In this "most famous of American epitaphs,"[2] as Carl Van Doren calls it, Franklin exemplifies his ability to make homely apostrophe the ironic mask of sophisticated cultural observation. When the individual existence inevitably falls into disrepair, according to Franklin's vision of things, it will be brought out in a new and more beautiful edition by a God who, like Franklin, is not only an author but a printer. He will both correct the errata of the first edition and make the new edition typographically elegant. In Franklin's epitaph salvation by faith in the regenerating grace of God becomes faith in the grammatical and verbal skills and in the printing shop know-how of a Deity who is both Man of Letters and Master Printer.

This symbolic representation of the God of Reason is as appropriate to the Age of the Enlightenment as the more familiar symbolism depicting Him as the Great Clock Maker. In proclaiming his adherence to deism, Franklin implies his rejection of the order of existence under which he had been reared, that of the New England theocracy. He suggests an awareness of his affiliation with an order of mind and spirit which as yet existed only in tentative ways in colonial America: an order additional to the realms of Church and State—the autonomous order of mind, the Republic of Letters, or a Third Realm, being made manifest as never before in Western civilization by the advancing technology of printing. Franklin's epitaph signifies the historical engagement of his whole career with the articulation of, and the expansion and consolidation of, the Third Realm in America.

I

Although the differentiation of the Third Realm in the Western symbolization of the orders of existence is difficult to document with any degree of exactitude, three phases in the history of this process may be briefly noted. In the first we discover the remoter origins of the Third Realm in a "Second Realm" of Grecian and Roman times. This was first instituted in the Athens of Socrates, Plato, and Aristotle, where a society of philosophers made a realm apart from the integral realm of religious and political power constituting the government of the City State. Later in the Rome

[2]Ibid., p. 123. Epitaph quoted on p. 124.

of Cicero and Virgil, the Second Realm was ideally constituted in
two visions of intellectual and literary community: the Stoic
vision of a cosmopolis of mind and the pastoral vision of Arcadia.
These were the invisible homelands of spiritual elites removed
from the conjoined politics and religion of the imperial state. The
more immediate origins of the Third Realm are to be located in
the intellectual and literary existence of the later Middle Ages.
Then, as a result of the differentiation of a struggle between
Church and State—a struggle, not previously known in history,
between a transcendent order of Being and the temporal order
of existence—a Republic of Letters emerged from the Republic
of Christ. In the grand design of the medieval papacy this Third
Realm would find its rationale in its function as the agency of the
assimilation and harmonization of Church and State; it would, as
Christopher Dawson remarks, "effect the intellectual organization of Christian civilization." The rise of the universities and the
complementary efforts centering in the quest of a unified Christian Republic, however, tended in the twelfth and thirteenth
centuries to place an emphasis on intellect and verbal skills that
disrupted the very quest. When the papacy began to seek to
elevate the Orders of Friars within the university corporations,
the secular clergy of the corporations resisted. The result was a
quarrel which, Dawson observes, "foreshadows the future secularization of Western culture." As the design of unity came more
and more into crisis, both as a result of pressures from within
the realm of the Church and of events from without, the secularization of mind was specifically, if ironically, foreshadowed
in the vision of Joachim of Flora. Joachim saw "the coming of a
new age, the Age of the Spirit and the Eternal Gospel in which
the Church will be renewed in the liberty of the spirit under the
leadership of the new order of Spiritual Contemplatives."[3] This

[3]Christopher Dawson, *Religion and the Rise of Western Culture* (New York:
Image Books, 1958), pp. 197, 204. The theory of history advanced by Eric Voe-
gelin is basic to an understanding of the Third Realm. See especially his *The
New Science of Politics: An Introduction* (Chicago: University of Chicago Press,
1952), pp. 107-32. Bizarre though they may be at times, the theories of Marshall
McLuhan must be recognized as highly significant. See in particular *The Guten-
berg Galaxy: The Making of Typographic Man* (Toronto: University of Toron-
to Press, 1962). Also see Lewis P. Simpson, "Literary Ecumenicalism of the
American Enlightenment," in *The Ibero-American Enlightenment,* ed. A. Owen
Aldridge (Urbana: University of Illinois Press, 1971), pp. 317-32; Simpson,

vision of Christendom dominated by a community of spiritually perfected monks—which harks back to the Stoic vision of a community or Second Realm of sages—could be adapted to variant concepts of secular intellectual order. It offered an image of an ecumenicalism of mind opposite to that afforded by the image of the university; and, as the latter image declined in importance, it supported the rise of a dominion of humanists as the Third Realm. This is the character of the Republic of Letters as it is represented, say, by a great Renaissance scholar such as Julius Caesar Scaliger, or in a less determinate but possibly more significant way by Erasmus. But the representation of the Third Realm became more various as the secularization of thought progressed and, with the loss of Latinity and the acceptance of the vernacular modes, its languages became manifold. It came to embrace the new science as well as classical humanism—although, it is of fundamental importance to observe, all activity of mind, down through the eighteenth century, continued to be viewed under the aspect of the use of letters. And through the eighteenth century this aspect continued to be seen as comprehensive. Meanwhile, the third, and most decisive, phase in the differentiation of the Republic of Letters was inaugurated by the invention of printing in the fifteenth century. This was eventually to result in the fragmentation and diffusion of the Third Realm; but the initial result was its expansion and growth in power. In the seventeenth and eighteenth centuries the Third Realm embraced a "classless" and crucial group of world historical men of letters: among them, Francis Bacon, Newton, Milton, Locke, Pope, Voltaire, Diderot, Hume, Franklin, John Adams, Jefferson. These intellectuals, together with numerous equal or lesser counterparts, over a period of a century and a half elaborated a comprehensive and searching inquiry into the meaning of the orders of existence. They shaped a Great Critique of Church and State.

The uniformity and repeatability of the printed word opened up the Great Critique, and the Third Realm as a whole, to the general society, creating a relationship between literacy and society never before known. Making for a more absolute distinc-

---

"Federalism and the Crisis of Literary Order," *American Literature*, 32 (November 1960), 253-66; and Simpson, "The Satiric Mode: The Early National Wits," in *The Comic Imagination in American Literature*, ed. Louis D. Rubin, Jr. (New Brunswick: Rutgers University Press, 1973), pp. 49-61.

tion between literacy and illiteracy—between the man of letters
and the man of no letters—the expansion of the Third Realm at
the same time introduced a distinction between degrees of literacy. This obtained between the man *of* letters and the man *with*
letters; between the man who practices the art of letters (the man
who has a vocation to letters) and persons whose use of letters
ranges from that of the "general reader" to that of the person who
cannot do more than inscribe his name. Under such cultural conditions the man *of* letters could seek to extend and enhance the
quality of the literacy of the man *with* letters; he could seek, up
to a point at least, to democratize the dominion in which the man
of letters functions. Or he could endeavor to maintain the dominion of letters as an exclusive, elitist polity of mind. In either
case the nature of literacy as a dominion became a historical
issue. In the first instance the liberation of the general mind
through the extension of the Republic of Letters was conceived.
In the second the confinement of letters and learning to the ap-
proximate scope it had achieved before the age of printing was
conceived. These polar impulses were present in seventeenth-
and eighteenth-century America, but Franklin's expression of
them has to be understood in connection with a special differentiation of the Third Realm under the conditions of New
England Puritanism.

The founding of Harvard College in 1636 embodied the Third
Realm in New England. Established to perpetuate a learned
ministry in the Puritan theocracy, Harvard descended from the
conception of the realm of letters and learning as the servant of
the autonomy of the Church. But Puritanism—and indeed the
whole dissenting and reformist movement lumped under the
head of Protestantism—had developed after humanism had become influential in the differentiation of the Third Realm. The
New England assimilation of Church and Letters showed increas-
ing evidences of humanistic leavening in the later seventeenth
century. Moreover, the New England clergy, in common with the
Puritan clergy as a whole, had originated as a learned class—an
intelligentsia—alienated from an official Church and State. The
Puritan clerics in England assumed the role, Michael Walzer says,
"of a clerical third estate," and in this capacity "tended to antici-
pate the intellectual and social changes characteristic of a secular
third estate."

Their "plain-speaking" and matter-of-fact style; their insistence upon education and independent judgment; their voluntary association outside the corporate church; their emphasis upon methodical, purposive endeavor, their narrow unemotional sense of order and discipline—all this clearly suggested a life-style very different from that of a feudal lord, a Renaissance courtier or even an Anglican archbishop. This new style was first tested on the margins and in the interstices of English society by men cut off from the traditional world, angry and isolated clerics, anxiously seeking a new order. It was by no means the entirely spontaneous creation of those sturdy London merchants and country gentlemen who later became its devoted advocates; it was something they learned, or rather, it was something some of them learned. The automatic burgher values—sobriety, caution, thrift—did not constitute the significant core of Puritan morality in the seventeenth century; the clerical intellectuals had added moral activism, the ascetic style, and the quality of high-mindedness and taught these to their followers.[4]

Among the followers was John Milton, the greatest exemplar of the intelligentsia of the laity among the Puritans. In *Areopagitica,* a classic document of the effort to establish the autonomy of the Third Realm, Milton defended the "truth" of the "commonwealth of learning" and attacked the fallacy of censorship imposed in the name of religious authority. In New England the life style of the third estate of Puritanism was more circumscribed than it was in England, but a basic disposition to respect the Republic of Letters is evidenced not only in the history of Harvard but in the development of the Boston-Cambridge community as the seat of the Enlightenment in New England. By the end of the first quarter of the eighteenth century, the rise of an independent order of secular men of letters was a possibility in the Boston world. One of its first manifestations was the appearance in 1721 of the *New England Courant,* edited by Benjamin Franklin's older brother James, who had returned to Boston after completing an apprenticeship to a London printer. During his connection with this little paper Benjamin Franklin began his personal representation of the Third Realm in New England and in America.

[4]Michael Walzer, *The Revolution of the Saints: A Study in the Origins of Radical Politics* (New York: Atheneum, 1968), p. 124.

II

Franklin's fundamental response to the Age of Printing was his discovery that it opened to the person of talent and ambition a self-education in letters and learning; his initiation into the actual techniques of the printing trade was no more than secondary to his unfolding vision of the intellectual resources of the printer's product and commodity.

The description of how he made himself into a scholar and writer is a noted passage in the *Autobiography*. Before he was twelve he began to read as chance and fortune brought books into his hands, investing whatever small sums of money he acquired in books, selling a set of Bunyan to purchase "R. Burton's historical collections," making his way through volumes of polemic divinity in his father's library when nothing else was available, reading "abundantly" in Plutarch, and eventually falling upon Defoe's *Essay on Projects* and Cotton Mather's *Essays to Do Good* (which he apparently assumed emphasized good works instead of saving grace). After he was apprenticed he secured books clandestinely from acquaintances among apprentices to Boston booksellers. ("Often I sat in my room reading the greatest part of the night, when the book was borrowed in the evening and to be returned early in the morning, lest it should be found missing or wanted.") At length a merchant, "an ingenious, sensible man, Mr. Matthew Adams," who often visited the printing house and who had "a pretty collection of books," invited the youth to make use of them. As he assiduously pursued the role of scholar, Franklin conceived the greater possibility of becoming a self-made writer. Having enjoyed some success with two Grubstreet ballads hawked about Boston only to be admonished by his father that "verse-makers were generally beggars," Benjamin turned to "prose writing" as the discipline offering the "principal means of Advancement." When he found his style "far short in elegance of expression, in method and in Perspicuity," as compared to that of his friend John Collins (with whom he had contested in a written debate), young Franklin — in an age when the fortuity of print had made history subject to the chance encounter between a mind and a book — "met with an odd volume of the *Spectator*."

It was the third. I had never before seen any of them. I bought it, read it over and over, and was much delighted with it. I thought the writing excellent and wished if possible to imitate it. With that view, I took some of the papers, and making short hints of the sentiment in each sentence, laid them by a few days, and then without looking at the book, tried to complete the papers again by expressing each hinted sentiment at length and as fully as it had been expressed before, in any suitable words that should occur to me.[5]

Franklin's imitation of the *Spectator* became more elaborate and arduous. To force himself to seek a greater variety in his vocabulary he transformed some of Mr. Spectator's stories into verse, and subsequently when he had "pretty well forgotten the prose, turned them back again." He scrambled the organization of thoughts and topics in the original papers and then sought to restore them to wholeness. Thus he taught himself "method in the arrangement of the thoughts." Franklin was, he says, "extremely anxious" to become "a tolerable English writer."[6] But in shaping himself into an author Franklin learned something more important to success than felicity of style. He learned that in the Age of Print a successful style involves a strategy of intimacy. This strategy is important in the *Spectator,* but it may be that the precocious Franklin discerned its significance earlier through his reading of a pure exemplification of the self-taught writer in the Age of Print, John Bunyan. That this could be the case is indicated in Franklin's recollection of an incident aboard a boat when he was on his way to Philadelphia to seek his fortune.

In crossing the bay we met with a squall that tore our rotten sails to pieces, prevented our getting into the kill, and drove us upon Long Island. On our way a drunken Dutchman who was a passenger, too, fell overboard; when he was sinking, I reached through the water to his shock pate and drew him up so that we got him in again. His ducking sobered him a little, and he went to sleep, taking first out

[5]Franklin, *Autobiography and Other Writings,* ed. Russel B. Nye (Boston: Houghton Mifflin, 1958), pp. 10-13. A detailed and interesting study of Franklin's journalistic career—from a point of view different from that stressed in the present essay—is to be found in James A. Sappenfield, *A Sweet Instruction: Franklin's Journalism as a Literary Apprenticeship* (Carbondale: Southern Illinois University Press, 1973).

[6]Ibid., p. 15.

of his pocket a book which he desired I would dry for him. It proved to be my old favourite author Bunyan's *Pilgrim's Progress* in Dutch, finely printed on good paper with copper cuts, a dress better than I had ever seen it wear in its own language. I have since found that it has been translated into most of the languages of Europe, and suppose it has been more generally read than any other book except, perhaps, the Bible. Honest John was the first that I know of who mixes narration and dialogue, a method of writing very engaging to the reader, who in the most interesting parts finds himself, as it were, admitted into the company and present at the conversation. Defoe has imitated him successfully in *Robinson Crusoe*, in his *Moll Flanders*, and other pieces; and Richardson has done the same in his *Pamela*, etc.[7]

The reader "admitted into the company, and present at the conversation." Franklin grasped one of the key motives of modern literacy: the identity of author and reader. Under an imperative of intimacy the postbardic author imitates the life of the "general reader." The author wears the guise of the reader, or, in a more intricate sense, disguises himself as the reader.

How well Franklin early comprehended the novel role of the writer in the extension of literacy through printing is illustrated in the *Dogood Papers*, which he contributed anonymously to the *New England Courant* in 1722, being then sixteen years old. Silence Dogood—a feminine Mr. Spectator carefully localized in manner and conversation—is a sophisticated persona; she is the youthful genius Franklin, the apprentice "leather-apron man" (printer), masquerading as the moral identity of the "common reader" in the age when secular moralism began to dominate post-theocratic New England. Silence begins her career as a writer by acknowledging the changing role of the author: "And since it is observed, that the Generality of People, now a days, are unwilling either to commend or dispraise what they read, until they are in some measure informed who or what the Author of it is, whether he be *poor or rich, old or young, a Schollar* or a *Leather Apron Man*, &c. and give their Opinion of the Performance, according to the Knowledge which they have of the Author's Circumstances, it may not be amiss to begin with a short account of my past Life and Present Condition, that the Reader may not

[7]Ibid., p. 19.

be at a Loss to judge whether or no my Lucubrations are worth his reading."[8]

Born on shipboard while her parents were emigrating from England to New England and almost at once orphaned when her father was swept overboard by a wave while he stood on the ship's deck rejoicing at her birth, Silence is the widow of a country minister to whom she was once apprenticed. The minister had acquired a library, "which tho' it was but small, yet it was well chose, to inform the Understanding rightly and enable the Mind to frame great and noble Ideas"; and in this little dominion of the mind Silence has become a student of letters. She is, one supposes, insufficiently liberated by present-day standards to be referred to as a "person of letters" instead of a "woman of letters." But such a term, used without pejorative implication, is a reasonably exact description of her status in society. Although Franklin conceives her as having womanly traits, she is relatively desexed and unclassed, a participant in her society and yet the observer of it. She is significantly aware furthermore, of her role as self-made author whose authority to write—the right to be an author—derives from her self-admission into the Third Realm. The most substantial essay Silence writes in her brief career is, as a matter of fact, a satirical commentary on the changing nature of this authority. This takes the form of a well-known satire on Harvard College in the fourth number of the *Dogood Papers.*

Silence, who has been urged by Clericus, a clergyman boarder in her home, to give her son an education at Harvard, soon afterward seeks her "usual Place of Retirement under the *Great Apple-Tree,*" where she falls asleep and has a dream about the Temple of Learning. The "stately edifice" turns out to be in fact a seat of dullness, inhabited by a tribe of students who, finding that learning is difficult and demanding, make the ascent to the throne of Learning only through following well-established modes of cheating. The chief import of the dream vision is "the extream Folly of those Parents, who, blind to their Childrens Dulness, and insensible to the Solidity of their Skulls, because they think their Purses can afford it, will needs send them to the Temple of Learning, where for want of a suitable Genius, they learn little more

[8]*The Papers of Benjamin Franklin,* ed. Leonard W. Labaree, et al. (New Haven: Yale University Press, 1959—), I:9. Referred to hereafter as *Papers.*

than how to carry themselves handsomely, and enter a Room
genteely, (which might as well be aquir'd at a Dancing-School,)
and from whence they return, after Abundance of Trouble and
Charge, as great Blockheads as ever, only more proud and self-
conceited." Silence, it is to be noted, does not discover in her
vision that college is a worthless institution, merely that its true
value is limited to the few who have the capacity for it. But the
poor among these few cannot gain admittance. The entrance to
the Temple of Learning must be made past two guards: Riches,
who admits applicants who can pay; and Poverty, who denies
those who cannot. The result is the bourgeois employment of the
college as a finishing school. And yet hidden in the satire on the
corruption of the true meaning of learning by money values is a
revelation of a profound change in the relation of letters and
learning to society. This occurs when Silence makes the curious
discovery that Learning "in awful State" on her "magnificent
Throne" is "very busily employ'd in writing something on a half
a Sheet of Paper." Upon inquiry Silence is told that Learning is
"preparing a Paper, call'd *The New-England Courant.*" Meanwhile:

> On her Right Hand sat *English,* with a pleasant smiling Counte-
> nance, and handsomely attir'd; and on her left were seated several
> *Antique Figures* with their Faces vail'd. I was considerably puzzl'd
> to guess who they were, until one informed me, (who stood beside
> me,) that those Figures on her left Hand were *Latin, Greek, He-
> brew,* &c. and that they were very much reserv'd, and seldom or
> never unvail'd their Faces here, and then to few or none, tho' most
> of those who have in this Place acquir'd so much Learning as to
> distinguish them from *English* pretended to an intimate Acquaint-
> ance with them. I then enquir'd of him, what could be Reason why
> they continu'd vail'd, in this Place especially: He pointed to the
> Foot of the Throne, where I saw *Idleness,* attended with *Ignorance,*
> and these (he informed me) were they, who first vail'd them, and
> still kept them so.[9]

This is a symbolization (it may well be the first in American
literature) of the expansion of the Third Realm—of the triumph
of the vernacular languages and of the periodical press. We note
that the satire does not present Learning as prostituted to the

[9]*Papers,* I: 15-16.

press. On the contrary, Learning has accepted her new role as printer-editor-publisher of a newspaper. If Idleness and Ignorance have veiled the learned languages, they have not veiled the goddess herself. She still reigns. The implication is that the center of the Republic of Letters has shifted from the university to the printing shop and the self-made author like Silence Dogood. Franklin does not imagine his little satire as a miniature *Dunciad* about the progress of dullness, a triumphant inversion of a progress of literature.[10] He offers a kind of celebration of the freeing of letters and learning from the authority of the university, realizing at the same time that this has occurred at the expense of a certain degradation of this initial embodiment of the polity of letters.

The implied elevation of the role of the self-made author in Silence Dogood is still more forcibly, if more subtly, suggested in the character and work of the philomath Richard Saunders, the editor of *Poor Richard's Almanack,* which Franklin commenced in Philadelphia ten years after the brief run of the *Dogood Papers.* A poverty-stricken countryman who is a lover of learning, Poor Richard enters into the business of writing after, as he says, his wife has threatened "to burn all my Books and Rattling-Traps (as she calls my Instruments) if I do not make some profitable Use of them for the Good of my Family." With the assurance of a printer than he will derive "some considerable share of the Profits," Poor Richard begins the publication of an almanac.[11] The result is a decided easing of his economic condition. His improved circumstances are more confirmed than denied when after a few years of publication Poor Richard is found complaining that the printer is running away with most of the profits of the almanac enterprise. The real meaning of Poor Richard's grievance lies in his qualification of it: the printer, he adds, "is a Man I have a great Regard for, and I wish his Profit ten times greater than it is."[12] This suggestion of the identity of Poor Richard and Franklin is more than waggish humor. In Poor Richard, Franklin the printer and Franklin the man of letters are united—more than they are in

[10]See Aubrey L. Williams, *Pope's Dunciad: A Study of Its Meaning* (Baton Rouge: Louisiana State University, 1955), esp. pp. 42-59.

[11]*Papers,* I: 311.

[12]*Papers,* II: 218.

Silence Dogood—as a representation of the expanding literacy of print. Poor Richard—purveyor of information, wit, and philosophical and scientific argument—embodies the domestication of the Third Realm in a world moving toward a democratic literacy inherent in the technology of print. (The full democratization of literacy would take place in the nineteenth century with the industrialization of the printing business.) Poor Richard, to be sure, recognizes the totality of the dominion of print and its replacement of the world of the manuscript and the oral mode; in four lines of doggerel verse which he offers as one of his quotations he says a farewell to the world of anonymous minstrels and bards and summarizes a world dominated by publication:

> If you wou'd not be forgotten
> As soon as you are dead and rotten,
> Either write things worth reading
> Or do things worth the writing.[13]

The opening up of the Third Realm is symbolized more dramatically in *Poor Richard's Almanack* of 1746 in the identification of Poor Richard with the tradition of the literary rural retreat.

> Who is *Poor Richard?* People oft inquire,
> Where lives? What is he? never yet the nigher.
> Somewhat to ease your Curiositee,
> Take these slight Sketches of my Dame and me.
>   Thanks to kind Readers and a careful Wife,
> With plenty bless'd, I lead an easy Life;
> My Business Writing; hers to drain the Mead,
> Or crown the barren Hill with useful Shade;
> In the smooth Glebe to see the Plowshare worn,
> And fill the Granary with needful Corn.
> Press nectareous Cyder from my loaded Trees,
> Print the sweet Butter, turn the Drying Cheese.
> Some Books we read, tho' few there are that hit
> The happy Point where Wisdom joins with Wit;
> That set fair Virtue naked to our View,
> And teach us what is *decent,* what is *true.*
> The Friend sincere, and honest Man, with Joy
> Treating or treated oft our Time employ.
> Our Table next, Meals temperate; and our Door

Op'ning spontaneous to the bashful Poor.
Free from the bitter Rage of Party Zeal,
All those we love who seek the publick Weal.[14]

The image of Poor Richard on his farm pleasantly engaged in
the "Business" of writing—while his wife tends to the agricultural
tasks—presents a striking variation of the ideal of literary retirement. Poor Richard's mercenary literary activity may be regarded as a violation of the integrity of the idealized pastoral
dominion of mind as this descends into eighteenth-century
literature from Virgil and Horace. The location of the almanac
maker's business in a pastoral setting may even be construed as a
pastoral strategy—that is, as affording a pastoral ratification of
Grubstreet, or bourgeois, enterprise. No doubt this motive exists
in the depiction of Poor Richard's Pennsylvania Twickenham.
But the complexity of Poor Richard must be taken into account.
He is not only a hack but a man of letters and a moral preceptor.
As a counselor in the use of money and time and the mutual
relation thereof, he presents the idea that financial independence
gained through intellectual work and the concept of pastoral
leisure defined in literary tradition can be brought together. Poor
Richard has earned his Arcadia, but it is not the less Arcadia. His
affluence enhances his moral independence.

III

Two years before he forsook an active part in the business of
printing and bookselling, Franklin established Poor Richard
securely in a symbolic home of the moral philosopher and man of
letters. This was, one surmises, a deliberate act on Franklin's
part. Removed from the city and worldly affairs, Poor Richard
becomes distinctly a voice carrying the authority of pastoral detachment. Although he identifies the literary vocation with that
of the farmer and thus appears as a common man articulating the
values of the common reader, Poor Richard is not fused with the
common mind. For all his expression of bourgeois-democratic

[14]*Papers*, III: 60. Important aspects of the retirement theme in the eighteenth
century are discussed in Maynard Mack, *The Garden and the City: Retirement
and Politics in the Later Poetry of Pope, 1731-1743* (Toronto: University of
Toronto Press, 1969).

attitudes, he speaks from the Third Realm. In his representation of the literary vocation, knowledge, wisdom, and wit do not spring from common literacy. He does not equate the man *of* letters and the man *with* letters.

There is more than a little justification in holding that, with whatever wry, ironic humor, Poor Richard symbolizes in provincial microcosm the cosmopolitan figure of letters and learning Franklin was becoming during the years between the almanac maker's inception and the middle of the eighteenth century. This was the figure David Hume acclaimed in 1762 when he learned of the American's imminent departure from the post he had held in England as colonial agent of Pennsylvania. At this time Hume wrote to Franklin:

> I am very sorry, that you intend soon to leave our Hemisphere. America has sent us many good things, Gold, Silver, Sugar, Tobacco, Indigo, &c.: But you are the first Philosopher, and indeed the first Great Man of Letters for whom we are beholden to her: it is our own Fault that we have not kept him: Whence it appears that we do not agree with Solomon that Wisdom is above Gold: For we take care never to send back an ounce of the later, which we once lay our Fingers upon.[15]

Hume's graceful but sincere compliment not only recognized Franklin as a peer of the Third Realm but also acknowledged the rise of the Republic of Letters in the colonial mind. But David Hume, it must be said, had little if any notion of the Franklin who wore the mask of Poor Richard. Hume, who was fearful lest his theoretical destruction of the soul be bruited among the common people, considered speculation and knowledge to be the proper province of the community of the lettered—"a closed and interlocked system of mutual admiration and criticism," as Basil Willey described it. Hume knew the Franklin who invited colonial Americans "in circumstances that set them at Ease, and afford Leisure" to "cultivate the finer Arts, and improve the common Stock of Knowledge" by forming a society of "Virtuosi or ingenious men." This would be called the American Philosophical Society, and it would be dedicated to maintaining "a

[15]*Papers*, X: 81-82.

constant Correspondence" on a great variety of subjects.[16] Hume scarcely understood that in the eighteenth century the self-articulation of the Third Realm through the correspondence of the learned could not be separated from the widening literacy of print.

Still less did Hume understand that in this expansion of literacy the Great Critique of Church and State was being translated into an active politics of literacy. This was a politics based not on the idea of a conquest of illiteracy—of the achievement of a universal literacy by means of a gross diffusion of elementary reading and writing skills—but on the concept of achieving a universal freedom of the educated secular mind by means of an extension of the Republic of Letters and an enhancement of its historical reality. This would be accomplished through the larger association of men of letters in a worldwide community created by a diffusion of pamphlets, magazines, and books and through an increase of the influence of men of letters. Which is to say, through an increase in the persons they can influence—in the number of men *with* letters who can be directed in the formation of an informed public opinion. The goal of the politics of literacy as it took shape in the Age of the Enlightenment was the domination of Church and State by the Third Realm, or—if it cannot be put quite so explicitly—the domination of history based on a cosmopolitan acquirement of a rational power over nature and man. The quest for such a dominion—for a moral government of the world by men of letters—was rooted in the faith that nature and man exist in a rational and (because it is rational) a moral universe; either nature or man is subject to explication in a rational employment of language.

As it became increasingly localized in a multiplicity of institutions such as the French Academy, the Royal Society, and the American Philosophical Society, the Republic of Letters became a realm operating within the conjoined realms of Church and State—in a loose but vital way a symbolic *imperium in imperio* in Western civilization. But the Third Realm became world historical in a definite sense only when it became operative and

---

[16]Basil Willey, *The Eighteenth Century Background: Studies in the Idea of Nature in the Thought of the Period* (Boston: Beacon Press, 1961), p. 123. Also, see page 122. *Papers*, II: 380-81.

active in the determination of events in specific historical situations, for example, that involving the relationship of the American colonies to the British Empire.

IV

Representing the American expression of the Third Realm as an *imperium in imperio* of the British Empire, Franklin assumed his full role as a world historical man of letters. Or, it is possibly more accurate to say, as a world historical printer. For in Franklin's view the vocation of the man of letters subsumed the vocation of the printer, that is, in the case of the printer as Franklin knew him: the printer in the eighteenth-century printing house, a combined technician, editor, publisher, and bookseller. From the beginning of his career Franklin conceived the representation of the Third Realm in the Age of Print to be the leather-apron man at the printing press screw. (As in the age of the manuscript the Third Realm had been represented by the figure of the copyist in the *scriptorum.)* Franklin's sense of the communication of the word was that it depends on the skill and integrity with which it is reproduced and disseminated. The politics of literacy—the examination of the truth of Church and State in a free debate of ideas—is singularly subject to how the printer regards his moral responsibility to his task. Franklin made a declaration of his moral commitment to printing in 1731, when, under pressure of an attack on his own press, he wrote "An Apology for Printers." Among the particulars of Franklin's defense of printers the following are exceptionally noteworthy:

> Printers are educated in the Belief, that when Men differ in Opinion, both sides ought equally to have the Advantage of being heard by the Publick; and that when Truth and Error have fair Play, the former is always an overmatch for the latter: Hence they chearfully serve all contending Writers that pay them well, without regarding on which side they are of the Question in Dispute.
>
> Being thus continually employ'd in serving both Parties, Printers naturally acquire a vast Unconcernedness as to right or wrong Opinions contain'd in what they print; regarding it only as the Matter of their daily labour: They print things full of Spleen and Animosity, with the utmost Calmness and Indifference, and with-

out the least Ill-will to the Persons reflected on; who nevertheless unjustly think the Printer as much their Enemy as the Author, and join them both together in their Resentment.

That it is unreasonable to imagine Printers approve of everything they print, and to censure them on any particular thing accordingly; since in the way of their Business they print such great variety of things opposite and contradictory. It is likewise as unreasonable what some assert, *That Printers ought not to print any Thing but what they approve,* since if all of that Business should make such a Resolution, and abide by it, an End would thereby be put to Free Writing, and the World would afterwards have nothing to read but what happen'd to be the Opinion of Printers.[17]

Yet another major particular in Franklin's list of ten in "An Apology for Printers" concerns the limits of a printer's moral tolerance.

That notwithstanding what might be urg'd in behalf of a Man's being allow'd to do in the Way of his Business whatever he is paid for, yet Printers do continually discourage the Printing of great Numbers of bad things, and stifle them in the Birth. I my self have constantly refused to print anything that might countenance Vice, or promote Immorality; tho' by complying in such Cases with the corrupt Taste of the Majority I might have got much Money. I have also always refus'd to print such things as might do real Injury to any Person, how much soever I have been solicited, and tempted with Offers of Great Pay; and how much soever I have by refusing got the Ill-will of those who would have employ'd me. I have hitherto fallen under the Resentment of large Bodies of Men, for refusing absolutely to print any of their Party or Personal Reflections. In this Manner I have made my self many Enemies, and the constant Fatigue of denying is almost insupportable. But the Publick being unacquainted with all this, whenever the poor Printer happens either through Ignorance or much Persuasion, to do any thing that is generally thought worthy of Blame, he meets with no more Friendship or Favour on the above Account, than if there were no Merit in't at all.[18]

A declaration of practice founded on his own experience, "An Apology for Printers" is as well a statement reflecting the experi-

---

[17] *Papers,* I:195.
[18] *Papers,* I:196.

ence of the Third Realm in its struggle for self-articulation in
history. It is both a practical and a symbolic statement: an an-
nouncement of a clear differentiation of the Third Realm in colonial American history. From this point on, a colonial press
—although it was always affected by governmental censorship—
would provide for the localization of the politics of literacy in
America. This is the development brilliantly described in Bernard Bailyn's *The Ideological Origins of the American Revolution.* Bailyn discovers a primary rationale of the American
Revolution in a colonial pamphlet literature which afforded "the
clarification and consolidation under the pressure of events of a
view of the world and of America's place in it." This literature
(Bailyn does not discuss it in quite the same terms used here) was
an offshoot of the expansion of the Third Realm in the England
of the Commonwealth and of the Glorious Revolution. These
were the ages of Milton, James Harrington, Henry Neville, and
Algernon Sidney. The diffusion of the politics of literacy by these
men of letters and "heroes of liberty" was carried further by
their inheritors in the early eighteenth century. Among these
were John Trenchard, Thomas Gordon, Bishop Hoadly, and
other pamphleteers who followed a "country" as opposed to a
London vision of government and social order and further
widened the influence of the Third Realm. Reprinted by American printers, the English pamphleteers became the core of an
American pamphlet literature that advanced the tendency to
democratize the mind and prepared the way for the Revolution,
not to speak of sustaining it once it began.[19]

Unifying the roles of printer and man of letters like no other
figure in the eighteenth century, Franklin expressed the harmony
and power—the hegemony—the Third Realm had achieved
three centuries after the invention of printing. His assertion of
the moral and intellectual power of the Republic of Letters is
integral to its evolvement into world historical meaning in the
Revolution and the founding of the new nation. And yet, like
Voltaire, though unlike more exuberant intellectuals such as
Condorcet, Franklin sensed the historical finitude of the Third

[19]Bernard Bailyn, *The Ideological Origins of the American Revolution*
(Cambridge: Belknap Press of Harvard University Press, 1967), pp. 22-54, 160-
229. Also, see Peter Gay, *The Enlightenment: An Interpretation* (New York:
Alfred A. Knopf, 1969), II:555-68.

Realm. His advocacy of the politics of literacy always conveys an indeterminate aura of ironic reservation about the quest for social order based on human wisdom, Franklin being constantly aware of the precarious balance between civilizational and barbaric impulses in man. His final statement about the liberty of the press is a pessimistic satire entitled "An Account of the Supremest Court of Judicature in Pennsylvania, Viz. The Court of the Press." In a time when the liberty of the press has become an unquestionable assumption of society, the sole recourse of the individual who is singled out for condemnation by its arbitrary decision may be, Franklin suggests, to take up a cudgel against printer and author. The violation of the civility of freedom by the press, in Franklin's satirical view at any rate, justifies a liberty of the bludgeon on the part of the victimized individual. But Franklin was disposed to think that man's capacity to create a literary and intellectual realm of existence expressed an ancient opposition to barbarism as inherent in his nature as the inclination to barbarism. He died believing that the God of the universe had conferred the possibility of "Government by human Wisdom"[20] on mankind, and that this possibility could be realized through the agency of the Third Realm. "God grant," he wrote almost at the end, "that not only the love of liberty, but a thorough knowledge of the rights of man, may pervade the nations of the earth, so that a philosopher may set his foot anywhere on its surface, and say, "This is my country.' "[21]

[20]"Motion for Prayers in Convention," in *Benjamin Franklin: Representative Selections,* ed. Frank Luther Mott and Chester E. Jorgenson (New York: American Book Company, 1936), p. 490. Franklin made this motion in the Constitutional Convention, June 28, 1787.

[21]Quoted in Nye, "Introduction" to *Autobiography and Other Writings,* pp. xvii–xviii.

Benjamin Franklin: The Making of
an American Character

by John William Ward

Benjamin Franklin bulks large in our national consciousness, sharing room with Washington and Jefferson and Lincoln.
Yet it is hard to say precisely what it means to name Franklin one
of our cultural heroes. He was, as one book about him has it,
"many-sided." The sheer variety of his character has made it
possible to praise him and damn him with equal vigor. At home,
such dissimilar Yankees as the laconic Calvin Coolidge and the
passionate Theodore Parker could each find reason to admire
him. Abroad, David Hume could say that he was "the first great
man of letters" for whom Europe was "beholden" to America. Yet
D.H. Lawrence, brought up, he tells us, in the industrial waste-
lands of midland England on the pious saws of "Poor Richard,"
could only "utter a long, loud curse" against "this dry, moral,
utilitarian little democrat."

Part of the difficulty in comprehending Franklin's meaning is
due to the opposites he seems to have contained with complete
serenity within his own personality. He was an eminently reasonable man who maintained a deep skepticism about the power of
reason. He was a model of industriousness who, preaching the
gospel of hard work, kept his shop only until it kept him and
retired at forty-two. He was a cautious and prudent man who was
a revolutionist. And, to name only one more seeming contradiction, he was one who had a keen eye for his own advantage and
personal advancement who spent nearly all his adult life in the

service of others. Small wonder that there have been various interpretations of so various a character.

The problem may seem no problem at all. Today, when we all know that the position of the observer determines the shape of reality, we observe the observer. If Franklin, seeing to it that the streets of Philadelphia are well lit and swept clean at a moderate price, that no fires rage, does not appeal to D. H. Lawrence, we tend not to think of Franklin. We think of Lawrence; we remember his atavistic urge to explore the dark and passionate· underside of life and move on. Franklin contained in his own character so many divergent aspects that each observer can make the mistake of seeing one aspect as all and celebrate or despise Franklin accordingly. Mr. I. Bernard Cohen, who has written so well on so much of Franklin, has remarked that "an account of Franklin...is apt to be a personal testament of the commentator concerning the America he most admires." Or contemns.

Yet there still remains the obstinate fact that Franklin could mean so many things to so many men, that he was so many-sided, that he did contain opposites, that he was, in other words, so many different characters. One suspects that here is the single most important thing about Franklin. Rather than spend our energies trying to find some consistency in this protean, many-sided figure, trying to resolve who Franklin truly was, we might perhaps better accept his variety itself as our major problem and try to understand that. To insist on the importance of the question, "Who was Benjamin Franklin?" may finally be more conclusive than to agree upon an answer.

The place to begin to ask the question is with the *Memoirs,* with the *Autobiography* as we have come to call them, and the place to begin there is with the history of the text. Fascinating in and of itself, the history of the text gives us an initial lead into the question of the elusiveness of Franklin's personality.

The *Autobiography* was written in four parts. The first part, addressed by Franklin to his son, William, was begun during some few weeks in July and August, 1771, while Franklin was visiting with his friend, Jonathan Shipley, the Bishop of St. Asaph, in Hampshire, England. Franklin was then sixty-five years old. As he wrote the first part he also carefully made a list of topics he would subsequently treat. Somehow the manuscript and list fell into the hands of one Abel James who eleven years later wrote Franklin, returning to him the list of topics but not the first part of the manuscript, urging him to take up his story once again. This was in 1782, or possibly early in January, 1783. Franklin was in France as one of the peace commissioners. He wrote the second part in France in 1784, after the achievement of peace, indicating the beginning and the ending of this short second part in the manuscript itself.

In 1785, Franklin returned to America, promising to work on the manuscript during the voyage. Instead he wrote three of his utilitarian essays: on navigation, on how to avoid smoky streetlamp chimneys, and on his famous stove. He did not return to his life's story until 1788. Then, after retiring from the presidency of the state of Pennsylvania in the spring, Franklin, quite sick, made his will and put his house in order before turning again to his own history. This was in August, 1788. Franklin was eighty-three years old, in pain, and preparing for death. The third part is the longest part of the autobiography, less interesting than the first two, and for many years was thought to conclude the manuscript.

In 1789, Franklin had his grandson, Benjamin Franklin Bache, make two fair copies of Parts I, II and III in order to send them to friends abroad, Benjamin Vaughan in England and M. le Veillard in France. Then, sometime before his death in April, 1790, Franklin added the last and fourth part, some seven and one-half manuscript pages, which was not included, naturally, in the fair copies sent abroad. For the rest, Mr. Max Farrand, our authority on the history of the text:

> After [Franklin's] death, the publication of the autobiography was eagerly awaited, as its existence was widely known, but for nearly thirty years the reading public had to content itself with French translations of the first and second parts, which were again translated from the French into other languages, and even retranslated into English. When the authorized English publication finally appeared in 1818, it was not taken from the original manuscript but from a copy, as was the preceding French version of the first part. The copy, furthermore, did not include the fourth and last part, which also reached the public in a French translation in 1828.
> ...the complete autobiography was not printed in English from

the original manuscript until 1868, nearly eighty years after Franklin's death.

The story is, as I have said, interesting in and of itself. The tangled history of one of our most important texts has its own fascination, but it also provides us the first clue to our question. Surely it must strike any reader of the *Autobiography* as curious that a character who speaks so openly should at the same time seem so difficult to define. But the history of the text points the way to an answer. All we need do is ask why Franklin wrote his memoirs.

When the Quaker, Abel James, wrote Franklin, returning his list of topics and asking "kind, humane, and benevolent Ben Franklin" to continue his life's story, "a work which would be useful and entertaining not only to a few but to millions," Franklin sent the letter on to his friend, Benjamin Vaughan, asking for advice. Vaughan concurred. He too urged Franklin to publish the history of his life because he could think of no "more efficacious advertisement" of America than Franklin's history. "All that has happened to you," he reminded Franklin, "is also connected with the detail of the manners and situation of a rising people." Franklin included James's and Vaughan's letters in his manuscript to explain why he resumed his story. What had gone before had been written for his family; "what follows," he said in his "Memo," "was written...in compliance with the advice contained in these letters, and accordingly intended for the public. The affairs of the Revolution occasioned the interruption."

The point is obvious enough. When Franklin resumed his story, he did so in full self-consciousness that he was offering himself to the world as a representative type, the American. Intended for the public now, his story was to be an example for young Americans, as Abel James would have it, and an advertisement to the world, as Benjamin Vaughan would have it. We had just concluded a successful revolution; the eyes of all the world were upon us. Just as America had succeeded in creating itself a nation, Franklin set out to show how the American went about creating his own character. As Benjamin Vaughan said, Franklin's life would "give a noble rule and example of self-education" because of Franklin's "discovery that the thing is in many a man's private power." So what follows is no longer the simple annals of Franklin's life for the benefit of his son. Benjamin Franklin plays his proper role. He becomes "The American."

How well he filled the part that his public urged him to play, we can see by observing what he immediately proceeds to provide. In the pages that follow James's and Vaughan's letters, Franklin quickly treats four matters: the establishment of a lending library, that is, the means for satisfying the need for self-education; the importance of frugality and industriousness in one's calling; the social utility of religion; and, of course, the thirteen rules for ordering one's life. Here, in a neat package, were all the materials that went into the making of the self-made man. This is how one goes about making a success of one's self. If the sentiments of our Declaration were to provide prompt notes for European revolutions, then Franklin, as the American Democrat, acted them out. Family, class, religious orthodoxy, higher education: all these were secondary to character and common sense. The thing was in many a man's private power.

If we look back now at the first part, the opening section addressed by Franklin to his son, William, we can·see a difference and a similarity. The difference is, of course, in the easy and personal tone, the more familiar manner, appropriate to a communication with one's son. It is in these early pages that Franklin talks more openly about his many *errata,* his "frequent intrigues with low women," and displays that rather cool and calculating attitude toward his wife. Rather plain dealing, one might think, at least one who did not know that William was a bastard son.

But the similarity between the two parts is more important. The message is the same, although addressed to a son, rather than to the world: how to go about making a success. "From the poverty and obscurity in which I was born and in which I passed my earliest years," writes the father to the son, "I have raised myself to a state of affluence and some degree of celebrity in the world." A son, especially, must have found that "some" hard to take. But the career is not simply anecdotal: "my posterity will perhaps be desirous of learning the means, which I employed, and which, thanks to Providence, so well succeeded with me. They may also deem them fit to be imitated." The story is exemplary, although how the example was to affect a son who was, in 1771, about forty years old and already Royal Governor of New Jersey is another matter.

The story has remained exemplary because it is the success story to beat all success stories: the runaway apprentice printer who rose to dine with kings; the penniless boy, walking down Market Street with two large rolls under his arms, who was to sit in Independence Hall and help create a new nation. But notice that the story does not deal with the success itself. That is presumed, of course, but the *Autobiography* never gets to the later and more important years because the *Autobiography* is not about success. It is about the formation of the character that makes success possible. The subject of the *Autobiography* is the making of a character. Having lifted himself by his own bootstraps, Franklin described it that way: "I have raised myself." We were not to find the pat phrase until the early nineteenth century when the age of the common man made the style more common: "the self-made man." The character was for life, of course, and not for fiction where we usually expect to encounter the made-up, but that should not prevent us from looking a little more closely at the act of creation. We can look in two ways: first, by standing outside the *Autobiography* and assessing it by what we know from elsewhere; second, by reading the *Autobiography* itself more closely.

A good place to begin is with those years in France around the end of the Revolution. It is so delicious an episode in plain Ben's life. More importantly—as Franklin said, one can always find a principle to justify one's inclinations—it is in these very years at Passy that Franklin, in response to James's and Vaughan's letters, wrote those self-conscious pages of the second part of the *Autobiography*. Just as he wrote the lines, he played them. As Carl Van Doren has written, "the French were looking for a hero who should combine the reason and wit of Voltaire with the primitive virtues celebrated by Rousseau. ...[Franklin] denied them nothing." This is the period of the simple Quaker dress, the fur cap and the spectacles. France went wild in its adulation and Franklin knew why. "Think how this must appear," he wrote a friend, "among the powdered heads of Paris."

But he was also moving with equal ease in that world, the world of the powdered heads of Paris, one of the most cosmopolitan, most preciously civilized societies in history. Although he was no Quaker, Franklin was willing to allow the French to think so. They called him *"le bon Quackeur."* The irony was unintentional, a matter of translation. But at the same time that he was filling the role of the simple backwoods democrat, the innocent abroad, he was also playing cavalier in the brilliant salon of Madame Helvétius, the widow of the French philosopher. Madame Helvetius is supposed to have been so beautiful that Fontenelle, the great popularizer of Newton, who lived to be one hundred years old, was said to have paid her the most famous compliment of the age: "Ah, madame, if I were only eighty again!" Madame Helvétius was sixty when Franklin knew her and the, classic anecdote of their acquaintance is that Madame Helvetius is said to have reproached him for not coming to see her, for putting off his long anticipated visit. Franklin replied, "Madame, I am waiting until the nights are longer." There was also Madame Brillon, not a widow, who once wrote to Franklin, "People have the audacity to criticize my pleasant habit of sitting on your knee, and yours of always asking me for what I always refuse."

Some, discovering this side of Franklin, have written him off simply as a rather lively old lecher. Abigail Adams, good New England lady that she was, was thoroughly shocked. She set Madame Helvétius down as a "very bad woman." But Franklin, despite his public style, was not so provincial. He appealed to Madame Brillon that he had spent so many days with her that surely she could spend one night with him. She mockingly called him a sophist. He then appealed to her charity and argued that it was in the design of Providence that she grant him his wish. If somehow a son of the Puritans, Franklin had grown far beyond the reach of their sermonizing. Thomas Hooker had thought, "It's a grievous thing to the loose person, he cannot have his pleasures but he must have his guilt and gall with them." But Franklin wrote Madame Brillon, "Reflect how many of our duties [Providence] has ordained naturally to be pleasures; and that it has had the goodness besides, to give the name of sin to several of them so that we might enjoy them the more."

All this is delightful enough, and for more one need only turn to Carl Van Doren's biography from which I have taken these anecdotes, but what it points to is as important as it is entertaining. It points to Franklin's great capacity to respond to the situation in which he found himself and to play the expected role, to prepare a face to meet the faces that he met. He could, in turn, be the homespun, rustic philosopher or the mocking cavalier, the witty sophist. He knew what was expected of him.

The discovery should not surprise any reader of the *Auto-biography*. Throughout it, Franklin insists always on the distinction between appearance and reality, between what he is and what he seems to be.

> In order to secure my credit and character as a tradesman, I took care not only to be in *reality* industrious and frugal, but to avoid all *appearances* of the contrary. I dressed plain and was seen at no places of idle diversion. I never went out a fishing or shooting; a book, indeed, sometimes debauched me from my work, but that was seldom, snug, and gave no scandal; and to show that I was not above my business, I sometimes brought home the paper I purchased at the stores, thro' the streets on a wheelbarrow. Thus being esteemed an industrious, thriving young man, and paying duly for what I bought, the merchants who imported stationery solicited my custom; others proposed supplying me with books, and I went on swimmingly.

Now, with this famous passage, one must be careful. However industrious and frugal Franklin may in fact have been, he knew that for the business of social success virtue counts for nothing without its public dress. In Franklin's world there has to be someone in the woods to hear the tree fall. Private virtue might bring one to stand before the King of kings, but if one wants to sit down and sup with the kings of this world, then one must help them see one's merit. There are always in this world, as Franklin pointed out, "a number of rich merchants, nobility, states, and princes who have need of honest instruments for the management of their affairs, and such being so rare [I] have endeavoured to convince young persons, that no qualities are so likely to make a poor man's fortune as those of probity and integrity."

Yet if one wants to secure one's credit in the world by means of one's character, then the character must be of a piece. There can be no false gesture; the part must be played well. When Franklin drew up his list of virtues they contained, he tells us, only twelve. But a Quaker friend "kindly" informed him that he was generally thought proud and overbearing and rather insolent; he proved it by examples. So Franklin added humility to his list; but, having risen in the world and content with the

degree of celebrity he had achieved, he could not bring himself
to be humble. "I cannot boast of much success in acquiring the
reality of this virtue, but I had a good deal with regard to the
appearance of it."

He repeats, at this point, what he had already written in the
first part of his story. He forswears all "positive assertion." He
drops from his vocabulary such words as "certainly" and "undoubtedly" and adopts a tentative manner. He remembers how
he learned to speak softly, to put forward his opinions, not dog-
matically, but by saying, "'I imagine' a thing to be so or so, or 'It
so appears to me at present.'" As he had put it to his son earlier,
he discovered that Socratic method, "was charmed with it,
adopted it, dropped my abrupt contradiction and positive argu-
mentation, and put on the humble enquirer." For good reason:
"this habit...has been of great advantage to me."

What saves all this in the *Autobiography* from being merely
repellent is Franklin's self-awareness, his good humor in telling
us about the part he is playing, the public clothes he is putting
on to hide what his public will not openly buy. "In reality," he
writes, drawing again the distinction from appearance, "there
is perhaps no one of our natural passions so hard to subdue as
pride; disguise it, struggle with it, beat it down, stifle it, mor-
tify it as much as one pleases, it is still alive and will every now
and then peep out and show itself. You will see it perhaps often
in this history. For even if I could conceive that I had completely
overcome it, I should probably be proud of my humility." Here,
despite the difference in tone, Franklin speaks like that other
and contrasting son of the Puritans, Jonathan Edwards, on the
nature of true virtue. Man, if he could achieve virtue, would inevitably be proud of the achievement and so, at the moment of
success, fall back into sin.

The difference is, of course, in the tone. The insight is the
same but Franklin's skeptical and untroubled self-acceptance is
far removed from Edwards' troubled and searching self-doubt.
Franklin enjoys the game. Mocking himself, he quietly lures us,
in his Yankee deadpan manner, with the very bait he has just
described. After having told us that he early learned to "put on
the humble enquirer" and to affect a self-depreciating pose, he
quotes in his support the line from Alexander Pope, "To speak,
though sure, with seeming diffidence." Pope, Franklin immedi-

ately goes on to say, "might have joined with this line that which he has coupled with another, I think less properly, 'For want of modesty is want of sense.'"

> If you ask why *less properly,* I must repeat the lines,

> > Immodest words admit of *no defence,*
> > *For* want of modesty is want of sense.

> Now is not the "want of sense" (where a man is so unfortunate as to want it) some apology for his "want of modesty"? and would not the lines stand more justly thus?

> > Immodest words admit *but* this defense
> > That want of modesty is want of sense.

> This, however, I should submit to better judgements.

Having been so bold as to correct a couplet of the literary giant of the age, Franklin quietly retreats and defers to the judgment of those better able to say than he. Having just described the humble part he has decided to play, he immediately acts it out. If we get the point, we chuckle with him; if we miss the point, that only proves its worth.

But one of the functions of laughter is to dispel uneasiness and in Franklin's case the joke is not enough. Our uneasiness comes back when we stop to remember that he is, as his friends asked him to, writing his story as an efficacious advertisement. We must always ask whether Franklin's disarming candor in recounting how things went on so swimmingly may not be yet another role, still another part he is playing. Actually, even with Yale's sumptuous edition of Franklin's papers, we know little about Franklin's personal life in the early years, except through his own account. The little we do know suggests that his way to wealth and success was not the smooth and open path he would have us believe. This leads us, then, if we cannot answer finally the question who Franklin was, to a different question. What does it mean to say that a character so changeable, so elusive, somehow represents American culture? What is there in Franklin's style that makes him, as we say, characteristic?

At the outset in colonial America, with men like John Winthrop, there was always the assumption that one would be called to one's appropriate station in life and labor in it for one's own good and the good of society. Magistrates would be magistrates and printers would be printers. But in the world in which Franklin moved, the magistrates, like Governor Keith of Pennsylvania who sends Franklin off on a wild-goose chase to England, prove to be frauds while the plain, leather-aproned set went quietly about the work of making society possible at all, creating the institutions—the militia, the fire companies, the libraries, the hospitals, the public utilities—that made society habitable. The notion that underlay an orderly, hierarchical society failed to make sense of such a world. It proved impossible to keep people in their place.

One need only consider in retrospect how swiftly Franklin moved upward through the various levels of society to see the openness, the fluidity of his world. Simply because he is a young man with some books, Governor Burnet of New York asks to see him. While in New Jersey on a job printing money he meets and makes friends with all the leaders of that provincial society. In England, at the coffeehouses, he chats with Mandeville and meets the great Dr. Henry Pemberton who was seeing the third edition of Newton's *Principia* through the press. As Franklin said, diligent in his calling, he raised himself by some degree.

The Protestant doctrine of calling, of industriousness in the world, contained dynamite for the orderly, hierarchical, social structure it was originally meant to support. The unintended consequence showed itself within two generations. Those who were abstemious, frugal, and hardworking made a success in the world. They rose. And society, rather than the static and closed order in which, in Winthrop's words, "some must be rich some poor, some high and eminent in power and dignitie; others meane and in subieccion," turned out to be dynamic, fluid and open.

If there is much of our national character implicit in Franklin's career, it is because, early in our history, he represents a response to the rapid social change that has remained about the only constant in American society. He was the self-made man, the jack-of-all-trades. He taught thirteen rules to sure success and purveyed do-it-yourself kits for those who, like himself, constituted a "rising" people. Franklin stands most clearly as an exemplary American because his life's story is a witness to the uncertainties about social status that have characterized our society, a society caught up in the constant process of change. The question, "Who was Benjamin Franklin?" is a critical question to ask of Franklin because it is the question to which Franklin himself is constantly seeking an answer. In a society in which there are no outward, easily discernible marks of social status, the question always is, as we put it in the title of reference works that are supposed to provide the answer, "Who's Who?"

Along with the uncertainties generated by rapid social mobility, there is another aspect to the difficulty we have in placing Franklin, an aspect that is more complex and harder to state, but just as important and equally characteristic. It takes us back again to the Puritans. In Puritan religious thought there was originally a dynamic equipoise between two opposite thrusts, the tension between an inward, mystical, personal experience of God's grace and the demands for an outward, sober, socially responsible ethic, the tension between faith and works, between the essence of religion and its outward show. Tremendous energy went into sustaining these polarities in the early years, but as the original piety waned, itself undermined by the worldly success that benefited from the doctrine of calling, the synthesis split in two and resulted in the eighteenth century in Jonathan Edwards and Benjamin Franklin, similar in so many ways, yet so radically unlike.

Franklin, making his own world as he makes his way through it, pragmatically rejects the old conundrum whether man does good works because he is saved, or is saved because he does good works. "Vicious actions are not hurtful because they are forbidden, but forbidden because they are hurtful," he decides, and then in an added phrase calmly throws out the God-centered universe of his forebears, "the nature of man alone considered."

Content with his success, blandly sure it must be in the design of Providence that printers hobnob with kings, Franklin simply passes by the problem of the relation between reality and appearance. In this world, appearance is sufficient. Humanely skeptical that the essence can ever be caught, Franklin decided to leave the question to be answered in the next world, if there proved to be one. For this world, a "tolerable character" was enough and he "valued it properly." The result was a common-sense utilitarianism which sometimes verges toward sheer crassness. But it worked. For this world, what others think of you is ·

what is important. If Franklin, viewed from the perspective of Max Weber and students of the Protestant ethic, can seem to be the representative, *par excellence,* of the character who internalizes the imperatives of his society and steers his own course unaided through the world, from a slightly different perspective he also turns out to be the other-directed character David Riesman has described, constantly attuned to the expectations of those around him, responding swiftly to the changing situations that demand he play different roles.

We admire, I think, the lusty good sense of the man who triumphs in the world that he accepts, yet at the same time we are uneasy with the man who wears so many masks that we are never sure who is there behind them. Yet it is this, this very difficulty of deciding whether we admire Franklin or suspect him, that makes his character an archetype for our national experience. There are great advantages to be had in belonging to a culture without clearly defined classes, without an establishment, but there is, along with the advantages, a certain strain, a necessary uneasiness. In an open and pluralistic society we have difficulty "placing" people, as we say. Think how often in our kind of society when we meet someone for the first time how our second or third question is apt to be, "What do you do?" Never, "Who are you?" The social role is enough, but in our more reflective moments we realize not so, and in our most reflective moments we realize it will never do for our own selves. We may be able to, but we do not want to go through life as a doctor, lawyer, or Indian chief. We want to be ourselves, as we say. And at the beginning of our national experience, Benjamin Franklin not only puts the question that still troubles us in our kind of society, "Who's Who?" He also raises the question that lies at the heart of the trouble: "Who am I?"

Benjamin Franklin

by D.H. Lawrence

The Perfectibility of Man! Ah heaven, what a dreary theme! The perfectibility of the Ford car! The perfectibility of which man? I am many men. Which of them are you going to perfect? I am not a mechanical contrivance.

Education! Which of the various me's do you propose to educate, and which do you propose to suppress?

Anyhow, I defy you. I defy you, oh society, to educate me or to suppress me, according to your dummy standards.

The ideal man! And which is he, if you please? Benjamin Franklin or Abraham Lincoln? The ideal man! Roosevelt or Porfirio Diaz?

There are other men in me, besides this patient ass who sits here in a tweed jacket. What am I doing, playing the patient ass in a tweed jacket? Who am I talking to? Who are you, at the other end of this patience?

Who are you? How many selves have you? And which of these selves do you want to be?

Is Yale College going to educate the self that is in the dark of you, or Harvard College?

The ideal self! Oh, but I have a strange and fugitive self shut out and howling like a wolf or a coyote under the ideal windows. See his red eyes in the dark? This is the self who is coming into his own.

The perfectibility of man, dear God! When every man as long as he remains alive is in himself a multitude of conflicting men.

Which of these do you choose to perfect, at the expense of every other?

Old Daddy Franklin will tell you. He'll rig him up for you, the pattern American. Oh, Franklin was the first downright American. He knew what he was about, the sharp little man. He set up the first dummy American.

At the beginning of his career this cunning little Benjamin drew up for himself a creed that should "satisfy the professors of every religion, but shock none."

Now wasn't that a real American thing to do?

"That there is One God, who made all things."

(But Benjamin made Him.)

"That He governs the world by His Providence."

(Benjamin knowing all about Providence.)

"That He ought to be worshipped with adoration, prayer, and thanksgiving."

(Which cost nothing.)

"But____" But me no buts, Benjamin, saith the Lord.

"But that the most acceptable service of God is doing good to men."

(God having no choice in the matter.)

"That the soul is immortal."

(You'll see why, in the next clause.)

"And that God will certainly reward virtue and punish vice, either here or hereafter."

Now if Mr. Andrew Carnegie, or any other millionaire, had wished to invent a God to suit his ends, he could not have done better. Benjamin did it for him in the eighteenth century. God is the supreme servant of men who want to get on, to *produce*. Providence. The provider. The heavenly storekeeper. The everlasting Wanamaker.

And this is all the God the grandsons of the Pilgrim Fathers had left. Aloft on a pillar of dollars.

"That the soul is immortal."

The trite way Benjamin says it!

But man has a soul, though you can't locate it either in his purse or his pocket-book or his heart or his stomach or his head. The *wholeness* of a man is his soul. Not merely that nice little comfortable bit which Benjamin marks out.

973.3092/

BENJAMIN

It's a queer thing is a man's soul. It is the whole of him. Which means it is the unknown him, as well as the known. It seems to me just funny, professors and Benjamins fixing the functions of the soul. Why, the soul of man is a vast forest, and all Benjamin intended was a neat back garden. And we've all got to fit into his kitchen garden scheme of things. Hail Columbia!

The soul of man is a dark forest. The Hercynian Wood that scared the Romans so, and out of which came the white-skinned hordes of the next civilization.

Who knows what will come out of the soul of man? The soul of man is a dark vast forest, with wild life in it. Think of Benjamin fencing it off!

Oh, but Benjamin fenced a little tract that he called the soul of man, and proceeded to get it into cultivation. Providence, forsooth! And they think that bit of barbed wire is going to keep us in pound for ever? More fools they.

This is Benjamin's barbed wire fence. He made himself a list of virtues, which he trotted inside like a grey nag in a paddock.

1
TEMPERANCE
Eat not to fulness; drink not to elevation.

2
SILENCE
Speak not but what may benefit others or yourself; avoid trifling conversation.

3
ORDER
Let all your things have their places; let each part of your business have its time.

4
RESOLUTION
Resolve to perform what you ought; perform without fail what you resolve.

5
FRUGALITY
Make no expense but to do good to others or yourself—i.e., waste nothing.

6
INDUSTRY

Lose no time, be always employed in something useful; cut off all unnecessary action.

7
SINCERITY

Use no hurtful deceit; think innocently and justly, and, if you speak, speak accordingly.

8
JUSTICE

Wrong none by doing injuries, or omitting the benefits that are your duty.

9
MODERATION

Avoid extremes, forbear resenting injuries as much as you think they deserve.

10
CLEANLINESS

Tolerate no uncleanliness in body, clothes, or habitation.

11
TRANQUILLITY

Be not disturbed at trifles, or at accidents common or unavoidable.

12
CHASTITY

Rarely use venery but for health and offspring, never to dulness, weakness, or the injury of your own or another's peace or reputation.

13
HUMILITY

Imitate Jesus and Socrates.

A Quaker friend told Franklin that he, Benjamin, was generally considered proud, so Benjamin put in the Humility touch as an afterthought. The amusing part is the sort of humility it displays. "Imitate Jesus and Socrates," and mind you don't outshine either of these two. One can just imagine Socrates and Alcibiades roaring in their cups over Philadelphian Benjamin, and Jesus looking at him a little puzzled, and murmuring: "Aren't you wise in your own conceit, Ben?"

"Henceforth be masterless," retorts Ben. "Be ye each one his own master unto himself, and don't let even the Lord put His spoke in." "Each man his own master" is but a puffing up of masterlessness.

Well, the first of Americans practised this enticing list with assiduity, setting a national example. He had the virtues in columns, and gave himself good and bad marks according as he thought his behaviour deserved. Pity these conduct charts are lost to us. He only remarks that Order was his stumbling block. He could not learn to be neat and tidy.

Isn't it nice to have nothing worse to confess?

He was a little model, was Benjamin. Doctor Franklin. Snuff-coloured little man! Immortal soul and all!

The immortal soul part was a sort of cheap insurance policy.

Benjamin had no concern, really, with the immortal soul. He was too busy with social man.

1. He swept and lighted the streets of young Philadelphia.

2. He invented electrical appliances.

3. He was the centre of a moralizing club in Philadelphia, and he wrote the moral humorisms of Poor Richard.

4. He was a member of all the important councils of Philadelphia, and then of the American colonies.

5. He won the cause of American Independence at the French Court, and was the economic father of the United States.

Now what more can you want of a man? And yet he is *infra dig.,* even in Philadelphia.

I admire him. I admire his sturdy courage first of all, then his sagacity, then his glimpsing into the thunders of electricity, then his common-sense humour. All the qualities of a great man, and never more than a great citizen. Middle-sized, sturdy, snuff-coloured Doctor Franklin, one of the soundest citizens that ever trod or "used venery."

I do not like him.

And, by the way, I always thought books of Venery were about hunting deer.

There is a certain earnest naïveté about him. Like a child. And

like a little old man. He has again become as a little child, always
as wise as his grandfather, or wiser.

Perhaps, as I say, the most complete citizen that ever "used
venery."

Printer, philosopher, scientist, author and patriot, impec-
cable husband and citizen, why isn't he an archetype?

Pioneer, Oh Pioneers! Benjamin was one of the greatest pioneers of the United States. Yet we just can't do with him.

What's wrong with him then? Or what's wrong with us?

I can remember, when I was a little boy, my father used to buy
a scrubby yearly almanac with the sun and moon and stars on the
cover. And it used to prophesy bloodshed and famine. But also
crammed in corners it had little anecdotes and humorisms, with a
moral tag. And I used to have my little priggish laugh at the
woman who counted her chickens before they were hatched and
so forth, and I was convinced that honesty was the best policy, also
a little priggishly. The author of these bits was Poor Richard,
and Poor Richard was Benjamin Franklin, writing in Philadelphia well over a hundred years before.

And probably I haven't got over those Poor Richard tags yet.
I rankle still with them. They are thorns in young flesh.

Because, although I still believe that honesty is the best policy,
I dislike policy altogether; though it is just as well not to count
your chickens before they are hatched, its still more hateful to
count them with gloating when they *are* hatched. It has taken me
many years and countless smarts to get out of that barbed wire
moral enclosure that Poor Richard rigged up. Here am I now in
tatters and scratched to ribbons, sitting in the middle of Benjamin's America looking at the barbed wire, and the fat sheep
crawling under the fence to get fat outside, and the watchdogs
yelling at the gate lest by chance anyone should get out by the
proper exit. Oh America! Oh Benjamin! And I just utter a long
loud curse against Benjamin and the American corral.

Moral America! Most moral Benjamin. Sound, satisfied Ben!

He had to go to the frontiers of his State to settle some disturbance among the Indians. On this occasion he writes:

> We found that they had made a great bonfire in the middle of the
> square; they were all drunk, men and women quarrelling and fight-
> ing. Their dark-coloured bodies, half-naked, seen only by the
> gloomy light of the bonfire, running after and beating one another

with fire-brands, accompanied by their horrid yellings, formed a scene the most resembling our ideas of hell that could well be imagined. There was no appeasing the tumult, and we retired to our lodging. At midnight a number of them came thundering at our door, demanding more rum, of which we took no notice.

The next day, sensible they had misbehaved in giving us that disturbance, they sent three of their counsellors to make their apology. The orator acknowledged the fault, but laid it upon the rum, and then endeavoured to excuse the rum by saying: "The Great Spirit, who made all things, made everything for some use; and whatever he designed anything for, that use it should always be put to. Now, when he had made the rum, he said: 'Let this be for the Indians to get drunk with.' And it must be so."

And, indeed, if it be the design of Providence to extirpate these savages in order to make room for the cultivators of the earth, it seems not improbable that rum may be the appointed means. It has already annihilated all the tribes who formerly inhabited all the seacoast. . . .

This, from the good doctor with such suave complacency, is a little disenchanting. Almost too good to be true.

But there you are! The barbed wire fence. "Extirpate these savages in order to make room for the cultivators of the earth." Oh, Benjamin Franklin! He even "used venery" as a cultivator of seed.

Cultivate the earth, ye gods! The Indians did that, as much as they needed. And they left off there. Who built Chicago? Who cultivated the earth until it spawned Pittsburgh, Pa?

The moral issue! Just look at it! Cultivation included. If it's a mere choice of Kultur or cultivation, I give it up.

Which brings us right back to our question, what's wrong with Benjamin, that we can't stand him? Or else, what's wrong with us, that we find fault with such a paragon?

Man is a moral animal. All right. I am a moral animal. And I'm going to remain such. I'm not going to be turned into a virtuous little automaton as Benjamin would have me. "This is good, that is bad. Turn the little handle and let the good tap flow," saith Benjamin, and all America with him. "But first of all extripate those savages who are always turning on the bad tap."

I am a moral animal. But I am not a moral machine. I don't work with a little set of handles or levers. The Temperance-silence - order - resolution - frugality - industry - sincerity - justice

- moderation - cleanliness - tranquility - chastity - humility key-board is not going to get me going. I'm really not just an automatic piano with a moral Benjamin getting tunes out of me.

Here's my creed, against Benjamin's. This is what I believe:

"That I am I."

"That my soul is a dark forest."

"That my known self will never be more than a little clearing in the forest."

"That gods, strange gods, come forth from the forest into the clearing of my known self, and then go back."

"That I must have the courage to let them come and go."

"That I will never let mankind put anything over me, but that I will try always to recognize and submit to the gods in me and the gods in other men and women."

There is my creed. He who runs may read. He who prefers to crawl, or to go by gasoline, can call it rot.

Then for a "list." It is rather fun to play at Benjamin.

1
TEMPERANCE

Eat and carouse with Bacchus, or munch dry bread with Jesus, but don't sit down without one of the gods.

2
SILENCE

Be still when you have nothing to say; when genuine passion moves you, say what you've got to say, and say it hot.

3
ORDER

Know that you are responsible to the gods inside you and to the men in whom the gods are manifest. Recognize your superiors and your inferiors, according to the gods. This is the root of all order.

4
RESOLUTION

Resolve to abide by your own deepest promptings, and to sacrifice the smaller thing to the greater. Kill when you must, and be killed the same: the *must* coming from the gods inside you, or from the men in whom you recognize the Holy Ghost.

5
FRUGALITY

Demand nothing; accept what you see fit. Don't waste your pride
or squander your emotion.

6
INDUSTRY

Lose no time with ideals; serve the Holy Ghost; never serve
mankind.

7
SINCERITY

To be sincere is to remember that I am I, and that the other man
is not me.

8
JUSTICE

The only justice is to follow the sincere intuition of the soul,
angry or gentle. Anger is just, and pity is just, but judgment is
never just.

9
MODERATION

Beware of absolutes. There are many gods.

10
CLEANLINESS

Don't be too clean. It impoverishes the blood.

11
TRANQUILLITY

The soul has many motions, many gods come and go. Try and
find your deepest issue, in every confusion, and abide by that.
Obey the man in whom you recognize the Holy Ghost; command
when your honour comes to command.

12
CHASTITY

Never "use" venery at all. Follow your passional impulse, if it
be answered in the other being; but never have any motive in mind,
neither offspring nor health nor even pleasure, nor even service.
Only know that "venery" is of the great gods. An offering-up of
yourself to the very great gods, the dark ones, and nothing else.

13
HUMILITY
See all men and women according to the Holy Ghost that is with-
in them. Never yield before the barren.

There's my list. I have been trying dimly to realize it for a long
time, and only America and old Benjamin have at last goaded me
into trying to formulate it.

And now I, at least, know why I can't stand Benjamin. He tries
to take away my wholeness and my dark forest, my freedom. For
how can any man be free, without an illimitable background? And
Benjamin tries to shove me into a barbed wire paddock and make
me grow potatoes or Chicagoes.

And how can I be free, without gods that come and go? But
Benjamin won't let anything exist except my useful fellow men,
and I'm sick of them; as for his Godhead, his Providence, He is
Head of nothing except a vast heavenly store that keeps every
imaginable line of goods, from victrolas to cat-o'-nine tails.

And how can any man be free without a soul of his own, that he
believes in and won't sell at any price? But Benjamin doesn't let
me have a soul of my own. He says I am nothing but a servant of
mankind—galley-slave I call it—and if I don't get my wages here
below—that is, if Mr. Pierpont Morgan or Mr. Nosey Hebrew or
the grand United States Government, the great US, US or SOME-
OFUS, manages to scoop in my bit, along with their lump—why,
never mind, I shall get my wages HEREAFTER.

Oh Benjamin! Oh Binjum! You do NOT suck me in any longer.

And why, oh why should the snuff-coloured little trap have
wanted to take us all in? Why did he do it?

Out of sheer human cussedness, in the first place. We do all
like to get things inside a barbed wire corral. Especially our
fellow men. We love to round them up inside the barbed wire
enclosure of FREEDOM, and make 'em work. *"Work, you free
jewel, WORK!"* shouts the liberator, cracking his whip. Benjamin,
I will not work. I do not choose to be a free democrat. I am absolutely a servant of my own Holy Ghost.

Sheer cussedness! But there was as well the salt of a subtler
purpose. Benjamin was just in his eyeholes—to use an English
vulgarism, meaning he was just delighted—when he was at Paris

judiciously milking money out of the French monarchy for the overthrow of all monarchy. If you want to ride your horse to somewhere you must put a bit in his mouth. And Benjamin wanted to ride his horse so that it would upset the whole apple-cart of the old masters. He wanted the whole European apple-cart upset. So he had to put a strong bit in the mouth of his ass. "Henceforth be masterless."

That is, he had to break-in the human ass completely, so that much more might be broken, in the long run. For the moment it was the British Government that had to have a hole knocked in it. The first real hole it ever had: the breach of the American rebellion.

Benjamin, in his sagacity, knew that the breaking of the old world was a long process. In the depths of his own under-consciousness he hated England, he hated Europe, he hated the whole corpus of the European being. He wanted to be American. But you can't change your nature and mode of consciousness like changing your shoes. It is a gradual shedding. Years must go by, and centuries must elapse before you have finished. Like a son escaping from the domination of his parents. The escape is not just one rupture. It is a long and half-secret process.

So with the American. He was a European when he first went over the Atlantic. He is in the main a recreant European still. From Benjamin Franklin to Woodrow Wilson may be a long stride, but it is a stride along the same road. There is no new road. The same old road, become dreary and futile. Theoretic and materialistic.

Why then did Benjamin set up this dummy of a perfect citizen as a pattern to America? Of course, he did it in perfect good faith, as far as he knew. He thought it simply was the true ideal. But what we *think* we do is not very important. We never really know what we are doing. Either we are materialistic instruments, like Benjamin, or we move in the gesture of creation, from our deepest self, usually unconscious. We are only the actors, we are never wholly the authors of our own deeds or works. It is the author, the unknown inside us or outside us. The best we can do is to try to hold ourselves in unison with the deeps which are inside us. And the worst we can do is to try to have things our own way, when we run counter to IT, and in the long run get our knuckles rapped for our presumption.

So Benjamin contriving money out of the Court of France. He was contriving the first steps of the overthrow of all Europe, France included. You can never have a new thing without breaking an old. Europe happens to be the old thing. America, unless the people in America assert themselves too much in opposition to the inner gods, should be the new thing. The new thing is the death of the old. But you can't cut the throat of an epoch. You've got to steal the life from it through several centuries.

And Benjamin worked for this both directly and indirectly. Directly, at the Court of France, making a small but very dangerous hole in the side of England, through which hole Europe has by now almost bled to death. And indirectly in Philadelphia, setting up this unlovely, snuff-coloured little ideal, or automaton, of a pattern American. The pattern American, this dry, moral, utilitarian little democrat, has done more to ruin the old Europe than any Russian nihilist. He has done it by slow attrition, like a son who has stayed at home and obeyed his parents, all the while silently hating their authority, and silently, in his soul, destroying not only their authority but their whole existence. For the American spiritually stayed at home in Europe. The spiritual home of America was, and still is, Europe. This is the galling bondage, in spite of several billions of heaped-up gold. Your heaps of gold are only so many muck-heaps, America, and will remain so till you become a reality to yourselves.

All this Americanizing and mechanizing has been for the purpose of overthrowing the past. And now look at America, tangled in her own barbed wire, and mastered by her own machines. Absolutely got down by her own barbed wire of shalt-nots, and shut up fast in her own "productive" machines like millions of squirrels running in millions of cages. It is just a farce.

Now is your chance, Europe. Now let Hell loose and get your own back, and paddle your own canoe on a new sea, while clever America lies on her muck-heaps of gold, strangled in her own barbed wire of shalt-not ideals and shalt-not moralisms. While she goes out to work like millions of squirrels in millions of cages. Production!

Let Hell loose, and get your own back, Europe!

The Autobiography of Benjamin Franklin: The Puritan Experimenter in Life and Art

by David Levin

The specter of Benjamin Franklin that continues to haunt us takes its shape not primarily from the critical interpretations of Max Weber and D. H. Lawrence but rather from Franklin's own work. It would be difficult to find a book that seems more widely understood, as a model of plain exposition of character, than *The Autobiography of Benjamin Franklin*. Everyone knows that this is the life of a self-made, self-educated man and that *Poor Richard's Almanac* was a best seller. Everyone knows that the penniless sixteen-year-old boy who first walked down the streets of Philadelphia with his pockets bulging with shirts and stockings, and with two great puffy rolls under his arms, worked so diligently at his calling that for him the promise of Scripture was fulfilled, and he one day stood before kings (He "stood before five," he wrote later, with characteristic precision, and sat down to dine with one.) We all know, too, that the Franklin stove and bifocals and the electrical experiments bear witness to Franklin's belief in lifelong education, and that it was because of his ability to explain clearly and persuade painlessly—even delightfully—that his international reputation soared higher than his famous kite.

Too often, however, we forget a few simple truths about this great man and his greatest works. We forget the chief purposes for which he wrote his autobiography, and the social system that led him to conceive such aims. Remembering the plainness of

"*The Autobiography of Benjamin Franklin:* The Puritan Experimenter in Life and Art." From *The Yale Review*, 53 (1964), 258-75. Copyright © 1964 by Yale University. Reprinted by permission of *The Yale Review*.

his expression, his clarity, we overlook his subtlety, his humor, and his qualifying statements. Above all, we forget that he was a writer, that he had a habit of creating characters. And so he takes us in. Some of us forget that Poor Richard is just as clearly Franklin's creation as is Mrs. Silence Dogood, the fictitious character through whom young Benjamin had published in his brother's newspaper in Boston; many of us forget that *The Way to Wealth,* Franklin's brilliantly successful collection of economic proverbs, is a humorous *tale* narrated by Poor Richard, who at first makes fun of himself and then reports the long speech made by another fictitious character named Father Abraham; and most of us overlook the crucial distinction, especially in the first half of Franklin's autobiography, between the *writer* of the book and the chief *character* he portrays.[1]

I do not mean to call Franklin's autobiography a work of fiction. We must refuse, however, to let its general fidelity to historical fact blind us to the author's function in creating the character who appears in the book. Franklin's first entry into Philadelphia may serve as an example. We are apt to consider the picture of that boy as a natural fact of history, as if no conceivable biographer could have omitted it. It merges in our experience with the myth that Horatio Alger exploited a century later, and with dozens of other pictures of successful men at the beginning of their careers: the country boy walking into the big city, the immigrant lad getting off the boat and stepping forth in search of his fortune. So grandly representative is this human experience that our current critical fashion would call it archetypal. But it was Franklin the writer who elected to describe this picture, and who made it memorable. He was not obliged to include it. He *chose* to make it represent an important moment in his life, and he chose to depict his young former self in particular

[1]Since this essay was first accepted for publication, two excellent studies of the *Autobiography* have emphasized this distinction. Although our arguments and citations inevitably converge, we differ sufficiently to support separate readings. See John William Ward, "Who Was Benjamin Franklin?" *The American Scholar,* XXXII (Autumn 1963), 541-53 [Reprinted as "Benjamin Franklin' The Making of an American Character" in Ward, *Red, White, and Blue: Men, Books and Ideas in American Culture* (New York: Oxford University Press, 1969), pp. 125-40, and present ed.] ; and Robert F. Sayre, *The Examined Self: Benjamin Franklin, Henry Adams, Henry James* (Princeton: Princeton University Press, 1964).

detail. His dirty clothes, his bulging pockets, and the huge rolls constitute nearly the only details respecting his personal appearance in the entire book. He might have omitted them, and he might have ignored the whole incident.

If we try to imagine what our view of Franklin might have been had he not written his autobiography, we will recognize that the author's conception of himself has considerably more literary significance than one can find in a single descriptive passage. Though the honest autobiographer refuses to invent fictitious incidents, he *actually creates himself as a character.* He selects incidents and qualities for emphasis, and discards or suppresses others. He portrays himself in relation to some other character (whom he also "creates" in this book), but refrains from portraying himself in relation to some others whom he once knew. He decides on the meaning of his life and the purpose of his book, and he selects traits, incidents, and characters accordingly. Obviously he cannot record everything that happened unless he spews forth every feeling, impulse, twitch that ever entered his mind or affected his senses. Indeed, the very conception of a happening requires some selection, some ordering of experience, and a point of view from which to perceive that order. D. H. Lawrence did not understand Franklin's autobiography, but he saw that it recognized a kind of order, and a view of the self, which imposed a planned control on natural feelings. "The ideal self!" he cried scornfully in his critique of Franklin.

> Oh, but I have a strange and fugitive self shut out and howling like a wolf or a coyote under the ideal windows. See his red eyes in the dark? This is the self who is coming into his own.
>
> The perfectibility of man, dear God! When every man as long as he remains alive is in himself a multitude of conflicting men. Which of these do you choose to perfect, at the expense of every other?
>
> Old Daddy Franklin will tell you. He'll rig him up for you, the pattern American. Oh, Franklin was the first downright American. He knew what he was about, the sharp little man. He set up the first dummy American.[2]

As we shall see later on, this gross caricature of "the sharp little man" reflects some imperfections in Franklin's ability to com-

---

[2]D.H. Lawrence, *Studies in Classic American Literature* (New York, 1923), pp. 13-14.

municate with ages beyond his own, and as we shall see even sooner, it suggests that Lawrence has not read Franklin carefully. For the moment, however, let us content ourselves with two observations in support of Lawrence's limited perception. First, Franklin's autobiography represents that kind of art in which the author tries to understand himself, to evaluate himself, to see himself, in a sense, from outside; it is a *portrayal* of the self rather than simply an *expression* of current feeling or an outpouring of those multiple selves that Lawrence celebrates. Old Daddy Franklin did indeed know what he was about. But the second observation must limit the praise in the first. The very terms in which Franklin expresses his admirable self-awareness limit his communication in a way that obscures the identity of the author. The technique of humor, and the disarming candor about techniques of influence and persuasion—these occasionally make us wonder which of several selves Benjamin Franklin is.

Franklin's art is deceptive. At first there may seem to be none at all. The book, written at four different times from 1771 to 1790,[3] the year Franklin died, is not only incomplete but loosely constructed; it is almost conversational in manner. It begins, indeed, as a letter to Franklin's son. It is episodic, anecdotal. Clearly, however, its narrative order includes two major divisions: the first half of the book describes his education, as he strives for a secure position in the world and for a firm character; the second half concentrates on his career of *public* service, though the account breaks off well before the American Revolution.

That simple pattern itself illustrates the most important fact about Franklin's autobiography. He not only creates an attractive image of himself but uses himself as a prototype of his age and his country. There are three essential ways in which he establishes this story of the self-made man securely in the broadest experience of his time. If we examine them with some care, we may understand his purposes and his achievement more clearly.

The first context is that of Puritanism, represented here by Franklin's admiration for John Bunyan's *Pilgrim's Progress* and

---

[3]There are many unsatisfactory texts of this unfinished masterpiece. The best edition generally available today is the Yale University Press edition of the Franklin papers. All quotations in this essay follow, with the publisher's permission, *The Autobiography of Benjamin Franklin,* ed. Leonard W. Labaree et al. (New Haven and London, 1964).

Cotton Mather's *Essays To Do Good.* Although Franklin says that he was converted to Deism by some anti-Deistic tracts in his Presbyterian father's library, we cannot overestimate the importance of his Puritan heritage, and his own account gives it due credit. (I refer, of course, not to the gross distortion suggested by the word "puritanical," the joy-killing and fanatical, but to that firm tradition that required every Christian to venture into this world as a pilgrim, doing right for the glory of God.) It is to this tradition that we owe Franklin's great proverb "Leisure is time for doing something useful," his emphasis on diligence in one's calling, the moral preoccupation that colors his view of ordinary experience. We see the Puritan influence in his acceptance of public duty, his constant effort to improve the community, his willingness at last to serve the local and international community without pay. When we remember that the Protestant ethic combines the profit motive with religious duty, we should remember that in Franklin's day (as in John Winthrop's before him) it also obliged one to use one's fortune, and one's own person, in public service.

The Puritan tradition, indeed, gave Franklin a more purely literary kind of model. By the time he was growing up there existed in both old and New England a fairly large body of personal literature that emphasized objective self-examination and the need to keep an objective record of divine Providence as it affected an individual life. One recorded one's daily life in order to evaluate one's conduct and also to find evidence of God's will in the pattern of events. It was the Puritan custom, moreover, to improve every opportunity to find moral instruction and signs of universal meaning in particular experience. Franklin himself describes and exemplifies this custom in an anecdote (not in the *Autobiography,* but in a letter) of a visit that he made in 1724 to the old Puritan minister Cotton Mather. As Franklin was leaving, he wrote later, Mather

> showed me a shorter way out of the house, through a narrow passage, which was crossed by a beam overhead. We were talking as I withdrew, he accompanying me behind, and I turning partly towards him when he said hastily, "STOOP, STOOP!" I did not understand him till I felt my head against the beam. He was a man that never missed any occasion of giving instruction, and upon this he said to me: "You are young, and have the world before you;

STOOP as you go through it, and you will miss many hard thumps." This advice, thus beat into my head, has frequently been of use to me, and I often think of it when I see pride mortified and misfortunes brought upon people by carrying their heads too high.[4]

One of the most successful devices that Franklin uses in his autobiography is this kind of symbolic anecdote, or parable; what brings Franklin's practice closer to Puritan preaching than to the parables in the Bible is his careful addition of a conclusion that drives home ;the point — the application or use — for those who might otherwise misunderstand it.

Before turning from Puritanism to a second quality of eighteenth-century experience, we should pause for another minute over the name of John Bunyan. For the first half of Franklin's autobiography, as Charles Sanford has said, represents a kind of pilgrim's progress. As his pious contemporaries Jonathan Edwards and John Woolman published accounts of their growth in Christian grace, so Franklin, acknowledging the aid of Providence, narrates the progress of a chosen, or at least fortunate, and often undeserving young man through a series of perils (including the valley of the shadow of death) to a relatively safe moral haven, if not to the Heavenly City. Others, we must remember, do not fare so well. A number of his early associates fall into one pit or another, and although Franklin tries to show what he did to save himself, so that others might profit by his example, he makes it perfectly clear that on several occasions he was so foolish that he too would have gone down had he not been preserved by Providence — or plain good luck.

It is this sense of the perils facing a young man in the free society of the new capitalism that brings me to the second of my three kinds of representativeness. Whether he was a Puritan or not, the young indentured servant, the young apprentice, the young artisan or farmer of Franklin's time, had to walk a perilous way in the world. And if, like a great many Americans, he was leaving his childhood community as well as the restraints and comforts of his childhood religious faith, when he came forth to make his way in the world, he faced those dangers with very little help from outside himself. He had precious little help in

[4]Benjamin Franklin to Samuel Mather, 12 May 1784.

the experience of others, for often his experience was new for the entire society. The mistakes he made did not entitle him to the protection of bankruptcy laws or the other comforts of our welfare state. They sent him to a debtor's prison, or subjected him to the permanent authority of a creditor. Franklin described plain economic fact as well as moral truth when he said, "It is hard for an empty sack to stand upright."

Thus one of Franklin's major purposes in the *Autobiography* was to instruct the young, not only by good example but by warning. Especially in his account of his youth, he presents himself repeatedly as the relatively innocent or ignorant young man in conflict with those who would take advantage of him. Much of the sharp dealing that annoys D. H. Lawrence and others occurs in this kind of situation. Franklin's older brother, exploiting and sometimes beating the young apprentice, tries to circumvent a court ruling against his newspaper by freeing young Benjamin and making him nominal owner of the paper; Benjamin takes advantage of the opportunity by going off to Philadelphia to strike out on his own. Samuel Keimer uses Franklin to train other printers so that Franklin's services may then be dispensed with; but Franklin plans to set up his own shop, and when he does, he prospers as Keimer fails.

Like the fiction of Daniel Defore, whom Franklin admired, and Samuel Richardson, whom he was among the first American printers to publish, Franklin's *Autobiography* indicates clearly that the relations between the sexes concealed some of the chief dangers to the young freeman's liberty. Luckily, he conceded, he escaped the worst consequences of occasional encounters with "low women"; but in a society that frankly recognized marriage as an economic contract he was almost entrapped by a clever pair of parents who seem to have counted on hoodwinking the young lad because he had to bargain for himself in a matter that required cooler heads. Franklin's account of the episode is priceless:

> Mrs. Godfrey [his landlady] projected a Match for me with a Relation's Daughter, took Opportunities of bringing us often together, till a serious Courtship on my Part ensu'd, the Girl being in herself very deserving. The old Folks encourag'd me by con-

tinual Invitations to Supper, and by leaving us together, till at
length it was time to explain. Mrs. Godfrey manag'd our little
Treaty. I let her know that I expected as much Money with their
Daughter as would pay off my Remaining Debt for the Printing-
house, which I believe was not then above a Hundred Pounds. She
brought me Word they had no such Sum to spare. I said they
might mortgage their House in the Loan Office. The Answer to
this after some Days was, that they did not approve the Match; that
on Enquiry of Bradford [another printer] they had been inform'd
the Printing Business was not a profitable one, the Types would
soon be worn out and more wanted, that S. Keimer and D. Harry
had fail'd one after the other, and I should probably soon follow
them; and therefore I was forbidden the House, and the Daughter
shut up. Whether this was a real Change of Sentiment, or only
Artifice, on a Supposition of our being too far engag'd in Affection
to retract, and therefore that we should steal a Marriage, which
would leave them at Liberty to give or withold what they pleas'd,
I know not: But I suspected the latter, resented it, and went no
more. Mrs. Godfrey brought me afterwards some more favourable
Accounts of their Disposition, and would have drawn me on again:
but I declared absolutely my Resolution to have nothing more to
do with that Family.

This anecdote is not among the most popular with modern
readers. It should be noticed, however, that people who owned
their house outright did not ordinarily leave their daughter
alone with a young man until they had some assurance of his
economic eligibility for marriage, and that these parents were not
worried about Franklin's ability to provide for their daughter
until he demanded the usual dowry. We should notice, too, that
the young Franklin who is described in this anecdote seems at
last to have obeyed his own feelings of resentment rather than the
economic interest that might have been served by allowing the
girl's parents to reopen negotiations.

But although he always prospers, the innocent young man is
not infallibly wise. Although he is never so roguish as Moll
Flanders, his confession appears to be remarkably candid. He
concedes that he was greatly deceived by the Governor of Pennsylvania, who sent him as a very young man to England, along
with supposed letters of recommendation and letters of credit
that never arrived. (That fool's errand, by the way, was probably the greatest peril of Franklin's young life, and he confesses

that he walked into it despite his father's clear warning.) He admits freely to motives and perceptions that we, along with most of his contemporaries, prefer to conceal. He thanks heaven for vanity, "among the other Comforts of Life," and admits that it is useful to cultivate not only the reality but the *appearance* of industry and humility. It was effective, he says, to carry his own paper stock through the streets in a wheelbarrow, so that people could see how hard he was willing to work. A book, he confesses, "sometimes debauch'd me from my Work; but that was seldom, snug, and gave no Scandal."

This apparent honesty leads us to the heart of the book. My third kind of representativeness, the most important of all, can be summed up in a single statement that appears near the end of the *Autobiography*. "This," Franklin wrote, "is the age of Experiments." It *was* the age of experiments, an age of empirical enlightenment, when every freeman might, if wary and lucky, learn by experience and test for himself. Franklin's greatest achievement in this book is that of characterizing himself repeatedly as a man of inquiry. He creates for us a convincing image of the inquiring man, self-educated, testing for himself, in morality, in business, in religion, in science. On almost every page we see some evidence of his willingness to learn. He contrives to reveal the vast range of his interests—from the pure science of electricity, to the effect of lading on the speed of merchant ships, to street lighting and street cleaning, to the value of learning modern Romance languages before trying to learn Latin—all these he contrives to reveal in anecdotes of questioning and discovery. And in anecdote after anecdote, the plain questioning of Benjamin Franklin in action applies an experimental test to theories and assumptions. As a young journeyman printer in England, he demonstrates to his fellow workmen that the customary beer is not necessary for the maintenance of strength: he drinks water, and carries more type than they can carry. Young Franklin and a friend agree that the one who dies first will prove the possibility of communicating from beyond the grave by getting in touch with the other who remains alive; but, Old Franklin the narrator reports, "he never fulfill'd his Promise." As a military commander at the start of the Seven Years' War with France, Franklin hears the zealous Presbyterian chaplain's complaint that the men do not attend religious services; he solves the problem

by persuading the chaplain himself to serve out the men's daily
rum ration just *after* prayers. "...and never," the narrator comments, "were Prayers more generally and more punctually attended. So that I thought this Method preferable to the Punish-
ments inflicted by some military Laws for Non-Attendance on
Divine Service."

Especially in the narrative of the early years, this wide-eyed
freshness of perception is perfectly compatible with the young
man's shrewdness, and it is nowhere more delightful than in his
depiction of some of the other chief characters in the book. One
of the most remarkable qualities in the book is the author's almost total lack of rancor. His brother James, Samuel Keimer,
Governor Keith, and General Edward Braddock — all these people may be said to have injured him; yet he presents them all with
the charitable curiosity of a man who was once interested in learning from his experience with them something about human
nature. I refer here not to the kind of curiosity that can be so
easily caricatured, the ingenious Yankee's humor that leads him
to tell us how he measured reports of the distance at which the
revivalist George Whitefield's voice might be heard. What I
mean to admire is the humorous *discovery* of another person's
strange faults. Consider the economy of this portrayal of Samuel
Keimer, whose faults are balanced against those of the young
Franklin:

> Keimer and I liv'd on a pretty good familiar Footing and agreed
> tolerably well: for he suspected nothing of my Setting up [for
> myself]. He retain'd a great deal of his old Enthusiasms, and lov'd
> Argumentation. We therefore had many Disputations. I us'd to
> work him so with my Socratic Method, and had trapann'd him [that
> is, tricked him] so often by Questions apparently so distant from
> any Point we had in hand, and yet by degrees led to the Point, and
> brought him into Difficulties and Contradictions that at last he
> grew ridiculously cautious, and would hardly answer me the most
> common Question, without asking first, *What do you intend to in-
> fer from that?* However it gave him so high an Opinion of my
> Abilities in the Confuting Way, that he seriously propos'd my being
> his Colleague in a Project he had of setting up a new Sect. He was
> to preach the Doctrines, and I was to confound all Opponents.
> When he came to explain with me upon the Doctrines, I found
> several Conundrums which I objected to unless I might have my
> Way a little too, and introduce some of mine. Keimer wore his

Beard at full Length, because somewhere in the Mosaic Law it said, *thou shalt not mar the Corners of thy Beard.* He likewise kept the seventh day Sabbath; and these two Points were Essentials with him. I dislik'd both, but agreed to admit them upon Condition of his adopting the Doctrine of using no animal Food. I doubt, says he, my Constitution will not bear that. I assur'd him it would, and that he would be the better for it. He was usually a great Glutton, and I promis'd my self some Diversion in half-starving him. He agreed to try the Practice if I would keep him Company. I did so and we held it for three Months. We had our Victuals dress'd and brought to us regularly by a Woman in the Neighbourhood, who had from me a List of 40 Dishes to be prepar'd for us at different times, in all which there was neither Fish Flesh nor Fowl, and the whim suited me the better at this time from the Cheapness of it, not costing us above 18*d.* Sterling each, per Week. I have since kept several Lents most strictly, Leaving the common Diet for that, and that for the common, abruptly, without the least inconvenience: So that I think there is little in the Advice of making those Changes by easy Gradations. I went on pleasantly, but poor Keimer suffer'd grievously, tir'd of the Project, long'd for the Flesh Pots of Egypt, and order'd a roast Pig. He invited me and two Women Friends to dine with him, but it being brought too soon upon table, he could not resist the Temptation, and ate it all up before we came.

Franklin's acute awareness that Keimer is a ridiculously pretentious, affected character does not prevent him from expressing some unsentimental sympathy for his former victim, or from hinting broadly that he himself now disapproves of giving himself diversion at the expense of others—although he might relish the chance to repeat the same experiment. We must remember, in reading this anecdote, that Franklin has previously told us of his decision some years later to abandon the Socratic method, because it had sometimes won him victories that neither he nor his cause deserved. And we must notice that his rational skepticism, his testing by experience, extends even to reason itself.

In an age of reason Franklin was not afraid to admit the limits of reason, nor did he hesitate in his autobiography to illustrate those limits by recounting an experience in which young Franklin himself is the only target of his humor. He used this device on several occasions, but one humorous anecdote is astonishing in its brilliance, for it not only establishes the author's attitude toward himself but describes his predicament in the key terms of

eighteenth-century psychology. The battle in young Franklin is
a battle between principle and inclination. The anecdote appears
immediately before the vegetarian experiment with Keimer.
During a calm on his voyage back from Boston to Philadelphia,
Franklin says,

> our People set about catching Cod and hawl'd up a great many.
> Hitherto I had stuck to my Resolution of not eating animal Food;
> and on this Occasion, I consider'd...the taking every Fish as a kind
> of unprovok'd Murder, since none of them had or even could do us
> any Injury that might justify the Slaughter. All this seem'd very
> reasonable. But I had formerly been a great Lover of Fish, and
> when this came hot out of the Frying Pan, it smelt admirably well.
> I balanc'd some time between Principle and Inclination: till I
> recollected, that when the Fish were opened, I saw smaller Fish
> taken out of their Stomachs: Then thought I, if you eat one an-
> other, I don't see why we mayn't eat you. So I din'd upon Cod very
> heartily and continu'd to eat with other People, returning only
> now and then occasionally to a vegetable Diet. So convenient a
> thing it is to be a *reasonable Creature,* since it enables one to find
> or make a Reason for every thing one has a mind to do.

Franklin gives us, then, the picture of a relatively innocent,
unsophisticated, sometimes foolish young man who confounds or
at least survives more sophisticated rivals. Consistently, the
young man starts at the level of testing, and he often stumbles
onto an important truth. We see his folly and his discoveries
through the ironically humorous detachment of a candid old
man, whose criticism of the young character's rivals is tempered
by the same kind of affectionate tolerance that allows him to see
the humor of his own mistakes. The wise old writer expects people to act selfishly but retains his affection for them. He leads us
always to consider major questions in terms of simple practical
experience, as when he tells us that he soon gave up converting
people to belief in Deism because the result seemed often to be
that they thus became less virtuous than before. Deism, he said,
might be true, but it did not seem to be very useful. Because he
assumed that at best people will usually act according to their
conception of their own true interest, because all his experience
seemed to confirm this hypothesis, and because metaphysical
reasoning often turned out to be erroneous, he concentrated on
demonstrating the usefulness of virtue.

It is right here, just at the heart of his most impressive achievement as an autobiographer, that Franklin seems to have made his one great error in communication. Many people, first of all, simply misunderstand him; he did not take sufficient account of the carelessness of readers. Many are completely taken in by the deceptive picture. So effective has Franklin been in demonstrating the usefulness of virtue through repeated anecdotes from his own educational experience, so insistent on effectiveness as a test of what is good in his own life, that many readers simply believe he has no other basis for deciding what is good. They simply conclude that the man who would say, "honesty is the best *policy*" will be *dis*honest if ever dishonesty becomes the best policy. Readers wonder what the man who tells them candidly that he profited by *appearing* to be humble hopes to gain by *appearing* to be candid.

If I were to follow Franklin and judge chiefly by the results, I would give up trying to clarify the misunderstanding, for I am sure that many readers will refuse to follow me beyond this point. Yet it seems to me important to understand Franklin's intention as clearly as possible, if only to measure properly the degree of his miscalculation or his inadequacy. Let us examine one other brief passage from the *Autobiography,* a statement describing Franklin's own effort to propagate a new set of religious beliefs, to establish a new sect which he proposed, characteristically, to call The Society of the Free and Easy. "In this Piece [a book to be called *The Art of Virtue*] it was my Design to explain and enforce this Doctrine, that vicious Actions are not hurtful because they are forbidden, but forbidden because they are hurtful, *the Nature of Man alone consider'd:* That it was therefore every one's Interest to be virtuous, who wish'd to be happy *even in this World.*"

I have stressed the qualifying phrases in this statement in order to emphasize the nature of Franklin's faith: *the nature of man alone considered;* everyone who wished to be happy *even in this world.* The doctrine of enlightened self-interest represents an important reversal—almost an exact reversal—of a sentence written by a sixteenth-century English Puritan named William Perkins, who in propounding the absolute sovereignty of God had declared: "A thing is not first of all reasonable and just, and then afterwards willed by God; it is first of all willed by God, and thereupon becomes reasonable and just." Yet Franklin's reversal does *not* say that discovering what is apparently to our interest is the only way of *defining* virtue. He, every bit as much as the Calvinist, believes that virtues must be defined by some absolute standard. Vicious actions, he says, *are forbidden*—by the benevolent authority of a wise God and by the universal assent, as he understood it, of wise men throughout history. But some actions *are* inherently vicious, whether or not they seem profitable.

Franklin's faith, then, professes that a true understanding of one's interest even in this world will lead one to virtue. Since the obvious existence of viciousness and folly in every society demonstrates that men do not yet practice the virtues on which most philosophers *have* agreed, finding a way to increase the practice of virtue—the number of virtuous actions—is a sufficiently valuable task to need no elaborate justification. And so the same Franklin who in the year of his death refused to dogmatize on the question of Jesus Christ's divinity because he expected soon to "have an opportunity of knowing the truth with less trouble," contented himself with questions of moral practice. His faith told him that the best way to serve God was to do good to one's fellow men, and he reasoned that just as all wise men preferred benevolent acts to flattery, so the infinitely wise God would not care very much to be flattered, but would prefer to have men *act* benevolently. He denied, however, that any man could ever *deserve* a heavenly, infinite reward for finite actions. He knew perfectly well the implications of his faith, but he saw no reason to worry very much about whether it was absolutely correct. For all his experience indicated that whether or not virtue and interest do coincide, no other argument but that of self-interest will persuade men to act virtuously, and even that argument will not always persuade them.

It is in this context that we must read Franklin's account of the thirteen-week course he gave himself in the Art of Virtue. D. H. Lawrence and other critics have overlooked the humorous self-criticism with which Franklin introduces the account. "It was about this time," Franklin says, "that I conceiv'd the bold and arduous Project of arriving at moral Perfection. . . . As I knew, or thought I knew, what was right and wrong, I did not see why I might not *always* do the one and avoid the other. But I soon found I had undertaken a Task of more Difficulty than I had imagined. While my *Attention was taken up* in guarding against one Fault, I was often supriz'd by another." Franklin, you will remember, listed the chief instrumental virtues under thirteen headings and at first devoted a week to concentrating especially on the habit of practicing one of the thirteen virtues. He made himself a chart, and in the daily period that he allotted to meditating the question "What Good have I done to day?" he entered a black mark for each action that could be considered a violation of the precepts. He worked to achieve a clear page. At thirteen weeks for each completed "course," he was able, he says, to go through four courses in a year. As he was surprised, at first, to find himself so full of faults, so he was pleased to find that he was able to decrease the number of his faulty actions. He endeavors to persuade us by pointing out that this improvement of conduct made him happier and helped him to prosper. But he makes perfectly clear the relative nature of his progress. He compares his method of attacking one problem at a time to weeding a garden, a task that is never really completed. He tells us not only that he later advanced to taking one course each year (with four weeks for each virtue), but also that he bought a book with ivory pages, so that he could erase the black marks at the end of one term and begin the course anew. The task was endless. Wondering about D. H. Lawrence's reading of Franklin, we may echo his own uncomprehending words: The perfectibility of man, indeed!

In trying to clarify Franklin's beliefs, I have not meant to absolve him of all responsibility for the widespread misunderstanding of his work. As I have already suggested, he invites difficulty by deliberately appearing to be more simple than he is, by choosing the role of the inquisitive, experimental freeman. By daring to reduce metaphysical questions to the terms of practical experience, he sometimes seems to dismiss them entirely, and he draws our attention away from the books that he has read. Thus, although he alludes to the most influential philosophical and psychological treatises of his age, and although he certainly read widely in every kind of learning that attracted his remarkably curious mind, he does not give this theoretical groundwork any important place in the narrative of his life. He mentions that he read John Locke at a certain point, and the Earl of Shaftesbury, and he says that this sort of education is extremely valuable. But in the narrative itself he is plain Benjamin Franklin, asking questions prompted by the situation. Even as he recounts, much later in the book, his successful correspondence with some of the leading scientists of England and the Continent, he underemphasizes his learning and portrays himself as a fortunate and plain, if skillful and talented, amateur.

This effect is reinforced by another quality of Franklin's literary skill, the device of humorous understatement. I have already cited one or two examples, as in his statement about answering the question of the divinity of Jesus. Similarly, he refers to the discovery that an effective preacher was plagiarizing famous English sermons as "an unlucky Occurrence," and he says that he preferred good sermons by others to bad ones of the minister's own manufacture. He repeatedly notices ridiculous incongruity by putting an apt word in a startlingly subordinate place and thus shocking us into a fresh, irreverent look at a subject that we may well have regarded in a conventional way. So he says that for some time he had been regularly absent from Presbyterian church services, "Sunday being my Studying-Day"; and he remarks that enormous multitudes of people admired and respected the revivalist George Whitefield, "notwithstanding his common Abuse of them, by assuring them they were naturally *half Beasts and half Devils.*" This is the method that Henry Thoreau later used in *Walden* when he declared that the new railroads and highways, which were then called internal improvements, were all external and superficial; it is the method Samuel Clemens employed through his narrator Huckleberry Finn, who says that at mealtime the widow Douglas began by lowering her head and grumbling over the victuals, "though there warn't really anything the matter with them." The device is often delightfully effective in negative argument, in revealing ludicrous inconsistency. But because it depends on an appeal to simple self-reliance, and often to a hardheaded practicality, it is not conducive to the exposition of positive, complex theory. The particular form of Franklin's wit, his decision to portray himself as an inquisitive empiricist, the very success of his effort to exemplify moral values in accounts of practical experience, his doctrine of enlightened self-interest, and the fine simplicity of his exposition — all these combine to make him seem philosophically more naïve, and practically more materialistic, than he is.

Yet this is a great book, and despite the limitations implicit in his pedagogical method, the breadth and richness of Franklin's character do come through to the reasonably careful reader. One chief means, of course, is the urbane yet warm tone of the wise old narrator, who begins by conceding that one of his reasons for writing an autobiographical statement to his son is simply the desire of an old man to talk about himself. We should also notice that although his emotional life is clearly beyond the bounds of his narrative purpose, he expresses an unmistakable affection, even in retrospect, for his parents, his brother, and his wife. His judgment is nowhere firmer or more admirable than in his account of the self-satisfied young Benjamin's return to taunt brother James, his former master, with the signs of the Philadelphia journeyman's prosperity. His record of his wife's life-long usefulness to him is not in the least incompatible with genuine affection for her. And in one brief paragraph citing as an argument for smallpox vaccination the death of his own son, "a fine Boy of 4 Years old," he reveals that his serenity could be rippled by the memory of an old grief.

We must remember, finally, that Franklin was one of the most beloved men of his time. The first American who was called the father of his country, he had no reason to feel anxious about the quality of what our own public-relations men would call his "image." He had retired at the age of forty-two to devote the rest of his long life to public service and scientific study; he was known internationally as a faithful patriot who had for decades defended the popular cause in almost every political controversy; he had been a great success at the French court, and he was a member of the Royal Society in England. With these sides of his character known so well, he had no reason to expect that his instructive *Autobiography* would be taken as the complete record of his character, or of his range as a writer. The polished *Bagatelles* that he had written in France, the brilliant ironic essays that he had published in England during the years just before the Revolution, the state papers that he had written in all seriousness as an agent of the Congress – all these formed a part of his public character before he completed his work on the *Autobiography*. He could not foresee that, in a romantic age in which many writers believed capitalism and practical science were overwhelming the human spirit, a novelist like D. H. Lawrence would make him a symbol of acquisitive smugness; nor could he foresee

that F. Scott Fitzgerald, lamenting in *The Great Gatsby* the betrayal of the great American dream, would couple Ben Franklin's
kind of daily schedule with a Hopalong Cassidy book, and would
imply that in the 1920's anyone who followed Franklin's advice
would have to be a stock-waterer or a bootlegger.

What Franklin represented in his day, and what we should see
in his greatest book, was something much more complex than this
stereotype. He was deceptively simple, to be sure; but his life and
his character testified to the promise of experience, the value of
education, the possibility of uniting fruitful public service with
simple self-reliance, the profitable conduct of a useful business
enterprise, and the free pursuit of knowledge in both pure and
practical science. His book remains an admirable work of art, and
its author still speaks truth to us as an admirable representative
of the Enlightenment.

Franklin and Spiritual Autobiography

by Daniel B. Shea, Jr.

Benjamin Franklin effectively settled the question whether his personal narrative might be thought of as spiritual autobiography when he referred to the manuscript as, simply, "Memoirs of my life." Nevertheless, there are persuasive reasons for considering Franklin's "Memoirs" against the background of early spiritual autobiography. Questions of sequence and development in American autobiography inevitably focus on Franklin. Is his the last Puritan autobiography, a translation of the narrative of salvation into secular terms? Or is Franklin the first authentic American autobiographer, displaying in his rise to success a mythic embodiment of the New World's possibilities? Should Franklin also be credited with a leap into modern autobiography, in his objectivity about himself and his implicit knowledge of the uses of a persona as narrator? To trace forward the lines leading from early spiritual autobiography to later representatives of the autobiographical mode in American literature is to encounter the many-sided Franklin, about whom all these things may be true at once. My own view is that in nineteenth-century America, Franklin was imitated more by deed than by autobiographical word, whereas the form and ingredients of early spiritual autobiography proved viable in a number of major contributions to American literature, among them *Walden, Song of Myself,* much of Emily Dickinson's poetry, and *The Education of Henry Adams.*

"Franklin and Spiritual Autobiography," in Daniel B. Shea, Jr., *Spiritual Autobiography in Early America.* Copyright © 1968 by Princeton University Press), pp. 234-248. Reprinted by permission of Princeton University Press.

I

The significance of Franklin's autobiography for American culture has been recognized from the beginning. Benjamin Vaughan, who had already edited some of Franklin's non-scientific writing in 1779, needed only Franklin's outline of his projected memoirs as a basis for observing: "All that has happened to you is also connected with the detail of the manners and situation of *a rising* people."[1] Vaughan's remark, made somewhat "at hazard" since he had not read the manuscript, has been echoed many times since 1783, frequently enough suggesting that other observers have written at a similar distance from the autobiographical text. Franklin's rise to affluence, his involvement in the struggle for independence, and his habit of inventing things may be generalized about in terms applicable to American cultural history and without recourse to the *Autobiography*. But like most American literature before 1830, Franklin's *Autobiography* derives major ingredients from England. Its Americanness cannot be discussed without noting that Ben Franklin, the archetypal apprentice studying hard to make good, is at least as much a product of English literature and society as of the American Dream. The Young Tradesman whom Franklin addressed in 1748 with the advice that "The Sound of your Hammer at Five in the Morning, or Nine at Night, heard by a Creditor makes him easy Six Months longer,"[2] could also learn from George Lillo's domestic tragedy, *The London Merchant*,[3] what befalls the apprentice who allows himself to be diverted from his task. The

[1]Franklin apparently wished Vaughan's letter included in his manuscript. See *The Autobiography of Benjamin Franklin,* ed. Leonard W. Labaree, Ralph L. Ketcham, Helen C. Boatfield, and Helene H. Fineman (New Haven, 1964), p. 135.

[2]"Advice to a Young Tradesman, Written by an Old One," *The Papers of Benjamin Franklin,* ed. Leonard W. Labaree and Whitfield J. Bell, Jr. (New Haven, 1961), III: 307.

[3]Lillo's drama was so successful that it went through eight editions from its first production in 1731 to 1740. There were also five pirated editions in the same period of time. See the editor's Introduction, *The London Merchant,* ed. William H. McBurney (Lincoln, 1965), pp. ix-xi. Staged ninety-six times in England during 1731 and 1747, the play was given to American audiences by at least two acting companies in the 1750's. See Arthur Hobson Quinn, *A History of the American Drama* (New York, 1923), pp. 8-9.

Young Tradesman who appears in the *Autobiography,* easing the minds of creditors as he wheels home his own supplies of paper, is a stock character following conventional advice. And although Lillo's George Barnwell is a very sentimental bad example, he has his equivalent in Franklin's characterization of his ne'er-do-well companions, Collins and Ralph, the one too drunk to join Franklin on a visit to the Governor of New York, the other a dissolute, would-be poet, likeable, but a burden and temptation to the earnest young printer. The affable "strumpets" Franklin is warned against by a grave, sensible Quakeress resemble more the "gallant dainty dame" who tempts Barnwell to destruction in the popular ballad[4] than the more complicated Mistress Millwood of Lillo's drama, but the family resemblance is close enough.

The two earliest reactions to the *Autobiography* on record refer Franklin's work to established traditions. Without specifying the body of writing he had in mind, Benjamin Vaughan remarked, "This style of writing seems a little gone out of vogue, and yet it is a very useful one."[5] Franklin's Quaker acquaintance, Abel James, compared the same portion of the narrative to the journals of public Friends, noting the great influence on youth of "Writings under that Class."[6] More recently, the first section of the *Autobiography,* which has the largest proportion of narrative, has been compared to a picaresque novel.[7] *Joseph Andrews* (1742), in particular, serves up two passages that indicate the transatlantic currency of certain types and ideas in the exemplary literature of the period and the immersion of the *Auto-*

---

[4]Lillo took his plot from an old ballad, first printed in 1650: McBurney, *The London Merchant,* p. xv. The ballad is printed as an appendix to this edition, pp. 86-89, and may have been known to Franklin, who composed several "wretched" pieces himself "in the Grubstreet Ballad Stile."

[5]Letter to Franklin, *Autobiography,* p. 138.

[6]Letter to Franklin, *Autobiography,* p. 134. James might well have been thinking of a journal like Thomas Chalkley's, which exhorts youth to sound mercantile virtues in language more familiar to us through Franklin's writing. Franklin printed Chalkley's *Works* in 1749. The anecdote Franklin uses in the *Autobiography* to rationalize his lapse from vegetarianism is mindful of Chalkley's observation: "Sailing in the great Deeps we saw the Wonders of the Lord, particularly in divers Kinds of Fish, they living upon one another in the Sea, the great Fishes on the small Ones; and Mankind too much resembles them in that Respect"(*Journal,* pp. 98-99).

[7]Robert Sayre, *The Examined Self: Benjamin Franklin, Henry Adams, Henry James* (Princeton, 1964), p. 18.

biography in those influences. One of Franklin's earliest lessons in self-reliance comes with the discovery that an offer by Sir William Keith to "set him up" will never be fulfilled, that in fact it was Keith's "known Character to be liberal of Promises which he never meant to keep" (p. 87). In telling this story, Franklin does away with the element of suspense from the outset in order to emphasize the youth's innocence and the vulnerability of a hope for future success which is based on gratuity rather than industry: "I believed him one of the best Men in the World." The revelation of his folly in voyaging to London on a promise is shocking to "a poor ignorant Boy," but the narrator speaks from larger experience in commenting, "It was a Habit he had acquired. He wished to please every body; and having little to give, he gave Expectation." The boy would have done well to read in *Joseph Andrews* the chapter in which Parson Adams has been promised a handsome living, lodging for the night, and horses for the next day by a gentleman who subsequently leaves word that he has gone on a long journey. In this case, an inn-keeper, rather than Franklin's Quaker merchant, confirms the gentleman's known character. The event justifies the suspicions of Joseph Andrews, who cites it as "a maxim" among the serving class in London "that those masters who promise the most perform the least."[8]

An even more exemplary portion of Fielding's work is Wilson's memoir of his life as a London dandy.[9] In the midst of debaucheries from which he was later reclaimed, Wilson had associated himself with a group who agreed to be guided by infallible human reason and by "a certain rule of right," propositions that seemed attractive until he saw one member steal another's wife and two others renege on their debts. Young Franklin is both leader and victim of such a group in the *Autobiography,* first convincing Collins and Ralph of the truth of his Deistic arguments, then, having been wronged by both men, "and recollecting Keith's conduct towards me, (who was another Freethinker) and my own towards Vernon and Miss Read which at times gave me great Trouble, I began to suspect that this Doctrine, tho it might be true, was not very useful" (p. 114).

[8]Henry Fielding, *The History of the Adventures of Joseph Andrews,* The Modern Library (New York, 1939), p. 205.

[9]Ibid., pp. 235-263.

Demonstrations of literary influence are, of course, notoriously untrustworthy, especially in the case of the autobiographer, to whom literary models may be entirely irrelevant. Presumably, Franklin mentions his "Inclinations for the Sea" and his father's apprehension that "I should break away and get to sea," because these details help along the narrative of his attempt to discover an appropriate vocation, not because Robinson Crusoe obeyed a similar inclination over similar paternal objections. However, when Franklin gave literary form to his narrative about a Young Tradesman he could scarcely escape from the presence of such characters as George Barnwell, Joseph Andrews, Robinson Crusoe, and John Bunyan's allegorical pilgrim, Christian, to whom the autobiographical Franklin has frequently been compared in his progress through the obstacles and temptations of a deceitful world. Whether, in any case, the figure of Benjamin Franklin embodies characteristics diffused through the society from which he emerged or was shaped out of the plentiful didactic literature of his time, he answers to a number of conventional expectations about young apprentices.

II

In England and in America, the Puritan background contributed to these expectations. Franklin's *Autobiography* may be taken as a type of all the secular covenants made between Americans and a Puritanism trimmed of its forbidding theology. As John Cotton told Franklin's Boston ancestors, the true Christian will not rest until he finds some "warrantable calling," by which, he explained, "we not only aim at our own, but at the public good." In the *Autobiography,* Franklin acknowledges this debt indirectly when he cites the influence of Cotton Mather's *Essays to Do Good* "on some of the principal future Events of my Life." Yet Franklin will never be mistaken for a Puritan spiritual autobiographer. He follows a Puritan custom in addressing his "Memoirs" to his son; like Cotton Mather he shares with his reader the methods which experience had proved most useful for attaining his ends; and like Thomas Shepard he desires to thank Providence for favorable dispensations toward him. But *The Autobiography of Benjamin Franklin* carries on no inquisition of the soul. The narrative records, but is not itself a quest, an act of potential discovery.

The work of John Bunyan which most attracted Franklin and which is most often associated with the *Autobiography* is *Pilgrim's Progress*, rather than the spiritual narrative, *Grace Abounding*. In the former, the perils of the journey. must be adequately characterized for the work to serve its purpose; but to show how Christian arrived finally at the Celestial City, these perils must be endurable and Christian's temptations conquerable. *Pilgrim's Progress* is a journey of discovery for Christian more than for Bunyan. One may wish to distinguish the speaker of *Grace Abounding* from the autobiographical character, but through most of the work the distinction is only technically valid. In a real sense, both may succumb to despair, both discover grace. *Pilgrim's Progress* (1678) not only follows *Grace Abounding* (1666) in time; its journey allegory is predicated upon the real quest undertaken in the autobiographical act.

This essential distinction is sometimes obscured by monolithic versions of Puritan autobiography: "For the Augustinian Christian, and the Puritan, personal history had order because God's ways were orderly and life was a period in which God revealed his order to his servants. For Franklin the possibilities of such revelation were exceedingly remote, and everything depended on each man's imposing some rational order on his daily life...or on his discovering order by his own investigations.[10] All Puritan autobiographers, we have assumed, found the same order in their lives, the indisputable order of the system that described the theology and mechanics of salvation. But in Puritan autobiography, attempted and realized arguments diverge so frequently for the evident reason that autobiographers were forced to seek answers to the question of grace, not in the system, but in the heart.

Anne Bradstreet and Thomas Shepard encourage posterity to holiness through all the means afforded by autobiography—with one exception; to stress emulation of the parent risked distracting one's children from their own quest for grace. Edwards' *Personal Narrative* argues the necessity of stringent criteria in judging spiritual experience, but it does not set forth an exemplar who

[10]Sayre, *The Examined Self*, pp. 34-35.

would be usefully imitated by spending "much time in viewing the clouds and sky, to behold the sweet glory of God in these things." Because the experience is carefully defined as an effect rather than a cause of grace, its imitation would be pointless. The pilgrim who moves through the first two sections of Franklin's *Autobiography* is himself exemplary in both a positive and negative sense, in his virtues and errata alike, and the Puritan autobiographer he resembles most in this respect was also, interestingly enough, the most prolific biographer of Puritan saints.

Cotton Mather works consistently to enlarge the exemplary features of his subjects both in "Paterna" and in the gallery of lives he drew up for the *Magnalia Christi Americana,* though he must counter vanity in writing about himself by making the character anonymous and by reducing him to his methods. Franklin too reveals more of his methods than of himself, and in recommending devices genially allows his name to be associated with the author of *Essays to Do Good.* The two men shared a common Enlightenment passion for projects in benevolence and membership in the Royal Society. In their respective styles—Mather's science would always support scripture—each had demonstrated an intention "to describe the *phenomena* of nature, to explain their causes...."[11] Similarly, both men preferred instruction which emphasized, as Franklin said, the "Means and Manner of obtaining Virtue," not the "mere Exhortation to be good."[12] In the age of Newton it was common knowledge that an effect, goodness, could not be expected from men who remained ignorant of

[11]Colin Maclaurin, *An Account of Sir Isaac Newton's Philosophical Discoveries* (1775), quoted in Carl Becker, *The Heavenly City of the Eighteenth-Century Philosophers* (New Haven, 1932), p. 62.

[12]Concentration on the means of effecting good was also appropriate for Mather as a pastor to Christians not subject to hierarchical authority and immersed in rapid social change. See David Levin's Introduction to his modern edition of *Bonifacius: An Essay upon the Good* (Cambridge, 1966), p. xv. Franklin, incidentally, would have read the portion of *Bonifacius* in which Mather, concealing his authorship of some advice on making pastoral visits, quoted from "the memorials of one who long since did so, and then left his PATERNA to his *son* upon it..." (p. 75). The running title, *Essays to Do Good,* identified this work, even in Franklin's time, rather than the more descriptive subtitle, "An Essay Upon the Good, that is to be Devised and Designed, By Those Who Desire to Answer the Great End of Life, and to Do Good While they Live."

its proper cause. The doctrine of free grace was preached as soundly by Cotton Mather as by his predecessors, but the *Essays to Do Good,* and their autobiographical equivalent, "Paterna," share with Franklin the elation of the New Science at being able to describe and participate in the great cause and effect system of Nature for the benefit of man and the greater glory of God.[13]

It is true that the amount of substantial empirical science in Franklin's *Autobiography* comes to very little. First readers must always be disappointed that the kite experiment receives only passing mention. But the utilitarian habit of mind flourishes everywhere as Franklin describes his probing for the agent of control, the cause whose effect is certain, and expresses his admiration for the success of men like George Whitefield, whose power is observable in his effects. "It was wonderful to see the Change soon made in the Manners of our Inhabitants," observes Franklin, before citing another and scarcely believable result of the preacher's power: "he finish'd so admirably, that I empty'd my Pocket wholly into the Collector's Dish, Gold and all" (pp. 175-177). Curious about the engine of his undoing, Franklin brushes aside questions of religious, social, or psychological causation to measure immediately the radius of Whitefield's voice and to compute the number of his auditors.

For Franklin the equivalent engine had been his prose, which he valued as a "principal means of my Advancement." As the narrative makes clear, control attained through the means of exercise and imitation leads eventually to significant results in one's personal fortune and in the affairs of others. A piece of his own writing, Franklin points out, created a clamor for paper money which the legislature could not neglect and brought the printing contract to his own house.[14] Whether or not it was true

---

[13]Mather exudes this feeling as he begins his work: "The *essay,* which I am now upon, is only to dig open the several *springs* of *usefulness;* which having once begun to run, will spread into *streams,* which no *human foresight* can comprehend. *Spring up, O well!*... Perhaps almost every proposal to be now mentioned, may be like a *stone* falling on a *pool; reader,* keep thy mind *calm,* and see, whether the effect prove not so! That one *circle* (and *service*) will produce another, until they extend, who can tell, how far? and they cannot be reckoned up." *Bonifacius,* p. 33.

[14]However, Franklin's memory shortened the distance between cause and effect. The editors of the *Autobiography* show that he received the contract to print currency, not immediately, but two years later, in 1731 (p. 124n).

that "Verse-makers were generally Beggars," as Josiah Franklin remarked on observing his son's interest in poetry, the experience of the *Autobiography* argues at least that poetry does not appear to be a cause of anything good, except perhaps better prose: "I approv'd the amusing one's self with Poetry now and then, so far as to improve one's Language, but no farther," observes Franklin (p. 90), echoing Mather's qualified approval of writing poetry "to sharpen your sense and polish your style for more important performances" in his *Manuductio ad Ministerium* (1726).

The Puritan aesthetic is at work here, of course, refusing to grant poetry the status of a "warrantable calling," but Franklin is less concerned with the sensualism of the imagination than its inefficacy. The temperance of the young apprentice dining on bread, raisins, and water makes no sermon on starving the body to save the soul, but it does make clear the sequence of good effects proceeding from control of appetite: money is saved, books are bought, which may be read, with a clearer mind, in the period otherwise spent taking a meal. Incident after incident recounts similar discoveries of power over nature as the protagonist extends his control over an increasingly large network of causation. The project for achieving moral perfection, which would have seemed a staggering implausibility in the context of Edwards' *Personal Narrative,* becomes an understandable and perhaps inevitable ambition for the protagonist of Franklin's *Autobiography.* To gain control of the causes of virtue in himself seems no vain hope in view of his past successes. At just this point, however, Franklin has propounded his autobiographical argument in its most extreme form. Having exhausted all his devices, the protagonist must finally accept the speckled ax of human fallibility. The experiment has been disappointing, but Franklin proffers his methods rather than his achievement as exemplary. A speckled ax cuts as well; method tends, however gradually, toward improvement. Sin may be an operable disease, even though the patient will always lack Adam's health.

III

The anecdote of the speckled ax belongs of course to the narrator, a witty, veteran traveler who stands apart from the developments of the narrative, measuring the protagonist against later experience. Understandably, modern readers have been especially alert to the recurring note of irony in the narrator's voice, but it is obviously overstating the case to suggest that Franklin never meant all he said about industry and frugality. His amusement at an innocent youth's estimate of human perfectibility does not hinder him from carefully reproducing his thirteen commandments, a sample chart of moral health, and the daily "Scheme of Employment." The passage informing the reader that "a little black Spot" imaged Ben Franklin's offenses invites a large measure of irony, and the narrator uses none. Instead, a pattern of unconscious symbolism suggests that both protagonist and narrator have forgotten what Puritans knew about human depravity. Franklin tells how the paper on which he recorded his faults "became full of Holes" with frequent erasure, making it necessary to transfer his chart to ivory leaves, "on which the Lines were drawn with red Ink that made a durable Stain, and on those Lines I mark'd my Faults with a black Lead Pencil, which Marks I could easily wipe out with a wet Sponge" (p. 155). There is no certainty in sin, which passes away, but the indelible red lines of method remain forever.

When irony appears, it signifies, to be sure, that the autobiographer is not wholly within his autobiography. Yet a reader has no direct sight of the wider life thus implied. Franklin draws a larger circle than the Puritan in delimiting experience fit for autobiography, but he defends his borders as carefully. Anecdotes that threaten to assert an independent reason for being are at last fashioned for display as exemplary versions of method and control. In successive paragraphs Franklin describes his relation with the widow from whom he rented in London and a visit to another of her boarders, the Roman Catholic anchoress who lived in the garret. The cameos in which Franklin recalls his conversation with these ladies impress the reader again with his ability to work effectively in miniature, scenically as well as in the pithy saying and the bagatelle. The brief sketches of the young American apprentice sharing an anchovy and a pint of beer with his landlady, charmed by her stories of the times of Charles II; later, inspecting the room of the seventy-year-old recluse who confessed her vain thoughts daily, taking in her solemn explanation of a picture of Veronica's handkerchief—these reminiscences finally justify their existence in Franklin's summary remarks, which call attention to the two shillings rent his landlady abated him for his companionship and to the illustration provided by the lady in the garret "on how small an Income Life and Health may be supported." With the sense of a duty to be performed, the didactic impulse edges aside others, nostalgic, curious, ironic, in order to carry on its argument.

It seems evident, then, that Franklin had no intention of allowing irony's counterpoint to become a counter-argument which would reduce the earnest apprentice to ludicrous sobriety and self-esteem. Irony forms part of a rhetoric sufficiently flexible to mediate between the demands of two very different audiences, the urbane readership that would set down copies of Voltaire in order to take up the memoirs of Franklin, and plain-minded readers like Abel James and Benjamin Vaughan. The harmony between Franklin's didacticism and his irony is well demonstrated in the characterization of Keimer, his first employer, whose failure as a printer coincides with Franklin's success. With obvious relish, Franklin relates the story of how Keimer, an enthusiast and dogmatist, agrees to practice vegetarianism with his apprentice. Eventually, flesh craves its kind, and Keimer invites Franklin and two ladies to share a roast pig with him, "but it being brought too soon upon the table, he could not resist the Temptation, and ate it all up before we came." Franklin treats Keimer's surrender as no more a vice in itself than his vegetarianism was a virtue. What Franklin enjoys is the vanquished dogmatist. He turns equal scorn on the Croaker, a local prophet of doom who maintains that Philadelphia is "a decaying Place... going to Destruction," and who must later buy property at five times its original worth. Yet the *Autobiography* offers no better example of delusion and the fixed idea than in its chief character, who goes penniless to England believing his own high opinion of himself is shared by the former governor, who prefers to rationalize vegetarianism when it is as easy to rationalize a taste for cod, and who conceives ambitious projects for moral perfection. Irony becomes at last the only device against an enthusiastic purveyor of devices and through its liberal use Franklin enforces his ban on "every Word or Expression in the Language that imparted a fix'd Opinion."

The history of "ambivalence toward Franklin and his legend"

pointed out by the Yale editors of the *Autobiography* is in part the history of attention to one pole or the other of Franklin's autobiographical argument. D. H. Lawrence, gifted with nearly infallible intuition in his *Studies of Classic American Writers,* lays bare the Franklinian code in the mechanistic non-soul of American materialism; but as a kind of dogmatist himself, Lawrence lacks patience to appreciate the Franklin who, failing to achieve moral perfection, reflected that after all "a perfect Character might be attended with the Inconvenience of being envied and hated" (p. 156). Exclusive emphasis on Franklin the ironist and shape-shifter, on the other hand, tends to neglect the powerful appeal of Franklin's *Autobiography* to the same desire that energizes the quest for grace, the hope of triumph over nature and limitation. Such a hope is universal and must account in the deepest sense for the popularity of Franklin's *Autobiography* abroad, though its proper setting has been the physical and economic wilderness of America. Neither a spiritual autobiography in the tradition of the Puritans and Quakers nor an American achievement in its formal characteristics, Franklin's *Autobiography* yet achieves a distinctly American mixture of naive perfectionism and skeptical empiricism, assuring its reader through autobiographical example that the world has yielded repeatedly to the onslaught of method, while reserving irony as a defense against hoping too much. Whatever we now find shallow or derivative in the *Autobiography* proved serviceable in its own time at least. If Franklin's example continues to survive its period of material service, it will do so on the strength of his argument that a man can make tolerable progress casting ahead of himself with reason, retaining only a settled bias against self-deceit.

Franklin and the Shaping
of American Ideology

by Michael T. Gilmore

Cotton Mather and Benjamin Franklin in their different ways foreshadow and illuminate the future development of American literature. Mather's entire career can be seen as an effort to breathe fresh life into the religion he inherited from his ancestors. This was the motive that impelled him to involve himself in the trials at Salem and to compose the witchcraft narratives in which he reaffirmed the essential rightness of the middle way. His heirs were the nineteenth-century romancers who undertook in their fiction to salvage the metaphysical vision of the first settlers of Massachusetts Bay. Franklin's purpose, in contrast, was not to preserve theological categories but to dispense with them, not to reclaim the temper of his ancestors but to secularize it. His heirs were instrumental in shaping the contours of American political and social thought, and he contributed to the emergence of an ideological conformity which the romancers opposed in their art. . . .

The "dying power of godliness"[1] mourned by Cotton Mather was interred by Poor Richard's proverbs and the *Autobiography*

[1]Cotton Mather, *Magnalia Christi Americana*, 2 vols. (1702; Hartford, 1820), 2: 285.

of Benjamin Franklin. Rejecting Calvinist theology, Franklin retained the Puritan social ethic and propounded it in his memoirs as a secular gospel, a gospel whose cardinal tenet was "Avoid Extreams" (p. 150).[2] The son of a professing member of Mather's own congregation, Franklin had planned to enter the ministry until financial hardship forced his father to withdraw him from grammar school. As an old man, he composed a new bible which replaced the Decalogue with the standard of utility and which was calculated to supplant his father's faith.

The mentality exemplified by Mather is represented in the *Autobiography* by Franklin's father Josiah. Franklin's ancestors, we learn at the beginning of his memoirs, were early converts to the Reformation, zealous in the opposition to popery and sufficiently Puritan in outlook to keep an English Bible in defiance of Queen Mary's edict. They remained within the Church of England, however, until the reign of Charles II, when Josiah broke with family tradition and turned nonconformist. In 1683, he emigrated to Massachusetts for religious reasons—conventicles being forbidden at home by law—and sometime after his arrival he was admitted to full communion in Boston's Old South Church. Even a cursory reading of the *Autobiography* confirms that Josiah was a devout Christian whose social preferences were unmistakably Puritan. He regularly attended public worship, gave his children a strict religious upbringing, and destined

[2]Benjamin Franklin, *Autobiography of Benjamin Franklin,* ed. Leonard W. Labaree et al. (New Haven: Yale University Press, 1964). Page references included in the text are from this edition. For other information on Franklin's life I have relied principally on Carl Van Doren, *Benjamin Franklin* (New York: Viking Press, 1938), and Alfred Owen Aldridge, *Benjamin Franklin: Philosopher and Man* (Philadelphia: J.B. Lippincott Co., 1965). Critical studies which I have found useful include J.A. Leo Lemay's "Benjamin Franklin," in *Major Writers of Early American Literature,* ed. Everett Emerson (Madison: University of Wisconsin Press, 1972), pp. 205-43; John F. Lynen's *The Design of the Present: Essays on Time and Form in American Literature* (New Haven: Yale University Press, 1969), pp. 119-52; David L. Minter's *The Interpreted Design as a Structural Principle in American Prose* (New Haven: Yale University Press, 1969), pp. 77-85; Robert F. Sayre's *The Examined Self: Benjamin Franklin, Henry Adams, Henry James* (Princeton: Princeton University Press, 1964), pp. 3-43; and, in particular, James A. Sappenfield's *A Sweet Instruction: Franklin's Journalism as a Literary Apprenticeship* (Carbondale: Southern Illinois University Press, 1973), pp. 178-214.

Benjamin as the tithe of his male offspring for the service of the church. Without being prosperous, he was never so poor as his son implied when the latter boasted of his own rise from "the Poverty and Obscurity in which I was born and bred" (p. 43). A modest tradesman, Josiah discouraged Benjamin's efforts at poetry on the grounds that "Verse-makers were generally Beggars" (p. 60). With the help of his wife Abiah, he managed to maintain "a large Family Comfortably"—according to the inscription on the tombstone which Benjamin himself erected in memory of his parents (p. 56). Nor was Josiah obscure for a man of his education and income. Prominent men in Boston respected his judgment and fairness and often appealed to him to mediate between contending parties. His character was captured in the epitaph supplied by his youngest son: "He was a pious and a prudent man" (p. 56).

Josiah was not, however, pious and prudent in equal degree, since for him the love of God took precedence over worldly moderation. His library was stocked with volumes of polemic divinity, and in matters of faith he showed little disposition to bend. Thus Benjamin recalled that when he lived under his father's care he was compelled to attend the church services which he afterward made it his custom to evade.

The inclusion of such material in the *Autobiography* establishes the religious and family background against which Benjamin was to revolt. The youthful Franklin portrayed in part one was intent upon repudiating the values of Boston and his immediate relations. He originally renounced *both* sides of Josiah's creed, the prudence as well as the piety, and became a skeptic and deist who engaged in "indiscriminate Disputations about Religion" which undermined his good standing with the churchgoers of his native city (p. 71). Instead of composing quarrels, he was at the center of them: he fought with both his brother and father, and incurred the enmity of the municipal authorities because of his penchant for controversy. When he quit Boston against his family's wishes, Benjamin assumed the first of the numerous identities he was to don throughout the period of his life covered in part one. He chose a persona which perfectly expressed the nature of his rebellion and forecast what he was increasingly to become: a sinner with an appetite for the lusts of the flesh. He brashly told the

captain of the sloop that carried him to New York that he had
gotten a girl pregnant and was fleeing in order to avoid having
to marry her.

As the flight by ship suggests, Benjamin tended to associate his
rejection of his father's values with the sea. According to the
Autobiography, his earliest differences with Josiah arose over his
desire to become a sailor, a desire which his father, having already lost one son in this fashion, was determined to prevent. He
was bound over to his brother James at the age of twelve precisely
in order to frustrate his urge to ship before the mast. Allusions
to water tend to crop up in the *Autobiography* whenever Benjamin is reprimanded by his father or the two of them disagree.
Every reader will recall the famous incident in which he was
punished for stealing some workmen's stones in order to build a
wharf. Even his penchant for poetry, of which Josiah cured him
by raising the spectre of beggary, fits into this pattern. He refers to two ballads of his own composition: one, entitled the *Light
House Tragedy,* contained the account of a drowning, while the
other consisted of a description of the seizure and execution of
the famous pirate, Blackbeard. And Franklin first mentions his
fondness for swimming in speaking of his refusal to enter his
father's business of chandlery: "I dislik'd the Trade and had a
strong inclination for the Sea; but my Father declared against it;
however, living near the Water, I was much in and about it, [and]
learnt early to swim well" (p. 53).

Franklin devoted himself to "forgetting Boston as much I
could" (p. 79), and he thoroughly identified his birthplace with
his father's beliefs. Once having made his way by sea to Philadelphia, he continued to shed his Puritan inheritance. His friendship with John Collins reflected this process inasmuch as Collins represented the first of the cautionary doubles in whom he
was to see his own transgressions magnified and with whom he
was to enjoy a brief intimacy. Collins was as bookish as Franklin
and the closest friend he had in Boston; when they moved to
Philadelphia, they lived together in the same house. Collins
borrowed money from Franklin which he was unable to repay;
Franklin broke into the money he was holding for Vernon and
only managed to repay it after several years had elapsed. But
Collins' deterioration—he was so often drunk that he was unable

to hold a regular job—was a constant reminder of Josiah's reproaches, and made a falling-out between the two young men inevitable.

In the printer Keimer, Franklin subsequently found an older model who was neither pious nor prudent, and in whose presence he freely indulged the habits his real father abhorred. Like Benjamin himself, Keimer was a poet, albeit an indifferent one, and he originally hired the young Bostonian to help him set the type for an elegy. He was also a religious enthusiast who invited Franklin to be his colleague in forming a new sect. Since he loved to quarrel, he and his employee had many arguments, the younger man invariably outwitting the older with his Socratic method. Josiah Franklin had little interest in food but rather made use of meal times to improve the minds of his children. Keimer, in contrast, was a glutton and womanizer who was incapable of resisting "the Flesh Pots of Egypt" (p. 89).

As he grew more intimate with Keimer, Franklin's relations with his real father apparently worsened. Josiah was dubious about his son's maturity and refused to lend him the money he needed to open a printing shop of his own. He admonished Benjamin to avoid the "lampooning and libelling to which he thought I had too much Inclination" (p. 83). The almost inevitable upshot was that Franklin once again took to the sea and sailed for England in the company of his friend James Ralph, thereby reversing the course that Josiah had followed when he fled the Old World in order to enjoy Congregational liberties in the New World. If Boston represented Puritanism and parental restraint, London was to become identified in the *Autobiography* with theological and personal irresponsibility. Franklin was further to associate such irresponsibility with his companion, Ralph, who now took the place of Collins as a cautionary double.

Ralph was an extreme version of the youthful Franklin. He was a poet, but unlike his friend who tried in vain to dissuade him, he was resolved to earn his livelihood by writing verse. His morals were as lax as his religious views, and when he went to England he left behind a wife and child whom he intended to desert. Thus he was doing in fact what Franklin had only pretended to do at the time he left Boston, when he made up the story about abandoning a pregnant girl. But the resemblance went even deeper than that, since in leaving Philadelphia for London, Franklin was actually deserting his wife-to-be, Deborah Read. The two young men were growing so close as to be virtually interchangeable. This process of identification was already well under way in Philadelphia where Franklin, at Ralph's request, had palmed off the latter's verses as his own. London simply accelerated the process, for once abroad the Americans proved to be "inseparable Companions" and took lodgings in the same house in Little Britain (p. 95). They acquired the habit of spending their evenings together at places of amusement, with the result that Franklin regularly exhausted his weekly earnings and was unable to save enough to pay for passage home. It was also in London that he composed the deist pamphlet, *A Dissertation on Liberty and Necessity, Pleasure and Pain,* which he later came to regard as an erratum. He dedicated the pamphlet to Ralph.

Eventually Franklin's identification with Ralph became all but complete. Unable to find employment in London, Ralph went to Berkshire to teach at a country school, and deeming such work beneath him, according to Franklin, "he chang'd his Name, and did me the Honour to assume mine" (p. 98). The man bearing the name Benjamin Franklin, in short, was now James Ralph; and soon after Ralph left the city, Franklin attempted familiarities with his friend's mistress, as if under the impression that the change of identities was more than a matter of names. When Mrs. T. repulsed his advances and informed her lover of them, Ralph terminated the friendship and used the breach as an excuse for refusing to repay the sums he had borrowed. Whereupon Franklin confessed that "in the Loss of his friendship I found myself reliev'd from a Burthen" (p. 99). The burden was the part of himself that identified with Ralph.

What ensued was a reaction to Ralph and Ralph's ways which impelled Franklin in the direction of asceticism and ethical precision. He now began to practice an austerity that far exceeded his father's and almost severed his ties to society. One incident in particular in the *Autobiography* shows Franklin in his new ascetic role. He declined to contribute a second time to his fellow workmen's fund for drink and was excommunicated for his singularity. The lesson he drew from the experience was "the Folly of being on ill Terms with those one is to live with continually"

(p. 100)—a lesson in prudence and accommodation that Josiah had endeavored to impress upon his son long ago.

Surely it is no accident that at this time Franklin gave up the lodgings he had formerly shared with Ralph in order to take rooms near a "Romish chapel" (p. 101). Having scouted the sins of excess in the presence of his friend, he now tested the extreme of other-worldliness represented by the monastic strain in Roman Catholicism. The connection between his needlessly stubborn stand for principle with his fellow compositors and the monkish excesses of the Catholic religion is highlighted by the fact that the workmen were accustomed, so Franklin disclosed in both the text and a footnote, to refer to the printing house as a "chapel" (p. 101). While situated at his new lodgings, moreover, he visited an English Catholic spinster who dwelt in the garret of the same house and who had vowed to "lead the life of a Nun as near as might be done" in a country without nunneries. She had donated her estate to charity and renounced her fellowship in society, limiting outside contact to a priest who confessed her each day. Franklin, though he admired her frugality, drew back from the otherworldly isolation which such extreme fidelity to principle produced.

He was now ready to return to Philadelphia and accept his father's social philosophy without adopting his religion. What he was on the verge of embracing, in other words, was the inner-worldly asceticism of Puritanism shorn of its theological frame-work. He made the transition all the more easily because he had been taken under the protection of a father figure who practiced the Puritan business ethic but appeared to have little interest in religion—albeit that he was nominally a Quaker. This agent of secular conversion was the merchant, Thomas Denham, whom the young man professed to love. Denham persuaded Franklin to accompany him to America, the prospects there being better than in England. He is described in the *Autobiography* almost exclusively in terms of his material achievement and financial probity, and Franklin delineates his character by recounting how he had recovered from bankruptcy and paid back every creditor the full amount outstanding with interest. The difference be-tween Denham and the elder Franklin is perfectly illustrated by the fact that the merchant emigrated to the New World in order to recoup his fortune, whereas Josiah had come for the sake of religion.

It was while he was with Denham at sea on the way to Philadelphia that Franklin drew up his plan for the conduct of his life, a plan, according to the *Autobiography,* which still regulated his behavior in old age. The plan itself is not printed in the book, and only the preamble and heads have been preserved, but these are sufficient to show that Franklin was more conversant with Puritan usage than is commonly assumed. He commented on the confusion and lack of fixed design which had characterized his life prior to 1726, the year of his return to America, and he added that since he was "now entering upon a new one," he wished to form a "scheme of action, that, henceforth, I may live in all respects like a rational creature." A new life founded on order and purpose, where formerly all had been chaos—the similarities to a conversion experience are evident. The difference, of course, is that grace played no part in Franklin's rebirth; the virtues he resolved to acquire were purely secular. With the exception of piety, however, they were identical to the virtues which he commemorated on the tombstone of his parents: thrift, honesty, industry, and a spirit of conciliation.[3]

Franklin summed up his relationship with Thomas Denham by saying that the merchant "counsell'd me as a Father" (p. 107), and in submitting to the older man's guidance he was implicitly making a partial peace with Josiah. The organization of the *Autobiography* supports this conclusion, for it reveals a new attitude on Franklin's part toward swimming, a sport he had associated with his rejection of his father's values. During the very period when he made up his mind to return to America, he was offered a handsome remuneration if he would teach swimming to a nobleman's two sons. The overture convinced him "that if I were to remain in England and open a Swimming School, I might get a good deal of Money"; but he was steadfast in his resolution to accompany Denham and informed the nobleman that he was unable to comply (pp. 105-6). While the Franklin of the memoirs rejected swimming as a physical activity, however, he began to relate it metaphorically to business in general and financial solvency in particular. In describing the printers with whom he

[3]Benjamin Franklin, *Papers of Benjamin Franklin,* 19 vols. to date, ed. Leonard W. Labaree et al. (New Haven: Yale University Press, 1959-), 1: 99-100.

worked at Watts's, for example, he dwelt on their addiction to beer and the expense of the habit: "And thus these poor devils keep themselves always under" (p. 100). Somewhat later, speaking of a trip he and Keimer had taken to New Jersey to print paper money, he said that the sum paid for the work enabled his employer "to keep his Head much longer above Water" (p. 112). As such examples suggest, swimming and material success were becoming synonymous in Franklin's mind at this period of his life. Reconciled by Thomas Denham to his father's Protestant ethic but not to his piety, he was hereafter to confine his "swimming" to business. In the *Autobiography,* he never again mentions his proficiency in the actual sport, and in part two he announces that he spent no further time "in Taverns, Games, or Frolicks of any kind" (p. 143).

The remainder of part one documents Franklin's transformation into Max Weber's rational capitalist. Repudiating his religious heresies, he took the lead in forming the Junto, a sect of an altogether different order from the one he had launched with Keimer. Membership in the Junto was limited to an apostolic twelve, and the rules strictly forbade warmth of expression or an argumentative tone. Without withdrawing from society, Franklin embarked on a regimen almost as ascetic as that of the English nun. He dressed plainly, allowed himself no diversions beyond an occasional book, and took care to acquire the appearance as well as the substance of an industrious and frugal character. He also undertook to repair his numerous "errata" by discharging his debt to Vernon—here the example of Denham could not have been far from his mind—and marrying Deborah Read.

Franklin's forsaking of his former ways is underscored by his experience with Meredith, the last of the doubles from whom he separates in the course of part one. Meredith resembled the Franklin of old in that he was a disappointment to his father because of the bad habits he seemed powerless to break. As with Collins, his besetting vice was drink, a weakness that threatened to drag Franklin into bankruptcy when the two friends entered into a business partnership. When Meredith persisted in his drinking to their mutual discredit, Benjamin dissolved the partnership and assumed sole control of the business. In casting off Meredith, he was figuratively shedding the vestiges of that part of himself which had first rebelled against Josiah nearly fifteen years earlier. Part one thus comes to an end with Franklin in full sympathy with his father's social values, a diligent and prudent young man bent on prosperity. In his own suggestive words, "I went on swimmingly" (p. 126).

Part one of the *Autobiography* belongs to the genre of confessional literature. In the manner, say, of Saint Augustine's *Confessions,* it tells the story of a young man's gradual disenchantment with sin—which Franklin called errata—and his painful conversion to the philosophy which was to guide him through life.[4] There are differences, however; most obvious is that Augustine converted to Christianity, whereas Franklin had as little use for conventional religion at the conclusion of part one as he had had at the beginning. In part two, accordingly, he addressed himself to the task of spelling out the precise nature of the creed to which he had given his allegiance, and he replaced Christianity with his table of virtues.

By virtue Franklin did not mean, as Jonathan Edwards meant, love of being in general. He meant instead a policy of enlightened self-interest such as Edwards, his exact contemporary, had defined as disguised self-love. He expounded his scheme for personal success through "the practice of Virtue, or what in the religious Stile are called Good Works" (p. 167)—an equation which the truly religious would have found abhorrent. Franklin wished to inspire the youth of America to emulate the industry, temperance, and frugality which had characterized his ascent to prosperity and eminence. He saw the Republic's collective destiny mirrored in his own success, and he was persuaded that his system of secular values was more relevant to the needs of "a *rising* people" than the outmoded Calvinism of churchmen like Edwards (p. 135).

There is no little significance in the fact that Franklin settled on thirteen virtues rather than ten or fifteen. The most obvious explanation is that four cycles of thirteen conveniently total fifty-two, the number of weeks in a year. According to Franklin, how-

---

[4]This accounts, incidentally, for the artful narrative technique to which writers on Franklin have recently called attention. It was a common practice in confessional literature for the author to present himself simultaneously from two points of view, looking back from the vantage of his altered consciousness upon his former unregenerate self.

ever, his original list contained only twelve virtues, and he did not add the thirteenth until admonished by a friend for insolence and pride. Only then did he include humility, giving as its precept "Imitate Jesus and Socrates" (p. 150).

Less than humble motives may well have entered into Franklin's calculations. He probably wanted to remind his readers of the thirteen colonies and to dramatize his identification of the nation with himself. To Franklin's contemporaries, who were steeped in the Scriptures, there was nothing unusual about the idea of representative men. They were familiar with the Old Testament method of recounting the affairs of an entire people as those of a single individual, the tribal patriarch. They had also been taught by their ministry that the community of believers has its corporate identity in Christ. And they knew from such classics of ecclesiastical history as Mather's *Magnalia* that the life of each saint exemplifies in miniature the collective epic of society. "I shall now invite my reader," Mather had written, "to behold at once the *wonders* of *New-England,* and it is in one Thomas Hooker that he shall behold them"[5]

In Mather's hagiographies, the hallmark of the saint is his conformity to Christ. In his table of virtues, Franklin adopted and radically revised this fundamental Christian concept. The twelve original virtues, with the addition of "Imitate Jesus," pointedly recall the apostles and the Savior, but Franklin's Christ was a very different figure from the Christ of Mather or Edwards. In an early piece entitled "Dialogue between Two Presbyterians," Franklin, speaking in the person of Socrates, ascribed to Jesus his own beliefs. "Our Savior," he argued, "was a Teacher of Morality or Virtue" who recommended faith only as "a Means to obtain that End." Thus was Christianity emptied of its spiritual significance. In the *Autobiography,* the historic ideal of *imitatio Christi* was transformed by Franklin into the injunction to imitate himself.[6]

In the threefold division of the Puritan sermon, as preached in America in the eighteenth century, the second section announced the minister's "Doctrine" and the third expounded the

[5]Mather, *Magnalia,* 1: 302-3.
[6]Franklin, *Papers,* 2: 29-30.

"Application" or "Uses." So with Franklin's *Autobiography*. By 1788, when he again resumed writing, he had returned to Philadelphia for good. Part three demonstrates the effectiveness of his creed in action, while it also shows a renewed acquaintance with American realities.

The decades covered in part three witnessed the greatest outpouring of religious fervor in the history of the colonies. It is apparent that the Great Awakening was not without its influence on Franklin. On the first page of the third installment, he proposed "Raising an United Party for Virtue" to be composed of the good and wise men of all nations, thus anticipating Jonathan Edwards's appeal for the visible union of God's people. Franklin candidly labeled his United Party for Virtue a sect, and the evangelical cast with which he endowed it obviously owed much to the pietistic stirrings of the age (pp. 161-63). Although the demands of business forced him to abandon his plan, he maintained a continuing interest in the revivals which swept America throughout the century. In part three, he makes a point of calling attention to the extraordinary number of revivalists who crossed his path. Six ministers appear in this section, and others are mentioned by name: with the exception of Edwards, they include some of the leading divines of the period, among them Gilbert Tennent and George Whitefield. It was against such figures that Franklin measured—and encouraged his readers to measure as well—his success as a doer of good.[7]

Even as he sought to divest himself of his orthodox heritage, Franklin remained in its debt. His secular teachings, as communicated through such vehicles as *Poor Richard's Almanack* (and the *Autobiography* itself), were calculated to foster the bourgeois habits of industry and thrift; for only by acquiring such habits, he believed, could the average citizen procure the modicum of wealth without which a virtuous carriage remained a shadowy ideal—"it being more difficult for a Man in Want to act always honestly" (p. 164). Franklin's reasoning invites comparison to the social thought of the emigrant Puritans, whose

---

[7]The most thorough treatment of Franklin's attitude toward the Calvinist clergy is Melvin H. Buxbaum's *Benjamin Franklin and the Zealous Presbyterians* (University Park: Pennsylvania State University Press, 1975). Buxbaum argues, wrongly I believe, that although Franklin long bickered with the religious establishment, he suppressed his anticlerical feelings in the *Autobiography*.

mentor William Perkins had long ago voiced a preference for the middle class. But whereas Perkins had believed that the middling sort—as opposed to beggars or the rich—were the more apt to be saved and numbered among the saints, Franklin was convinced that they were the backbone of a virtuous citizenry. This consideration took on special urgency when Franklin contemplated the future of America. Believing that the survival of freedom depended upon the virtue of a nation's people, he composed his most sustained panegyric on behalf of the middling folk, *Information for Those Who Would Remove to America*, in late 1782 or 1783, at a time when independence was assured. Prospective emigrants were showering him with enquiries about conditions in the New World. Franklin replied by picturing America as a land of labor and opportunity where a "general Mediocrity of Fortune" prevailed, and he warned away both the idle pauper and the useless aristocrat who had "no other Quality to recommend him but his Birth."[8] While such sentiments were commonplace enough among the French physiocrats who flocked to Passy, they had a precedent nearer to home in the literature of dissuasion that had issued from Plymouth during the early years of the settlement. The *Information for Those Who Would Remove to America*, with its paean to "Happy Mediocrity," can be read as an eighteenth-century restatement of Robert Cushman's 1621ᐧ discourse on "The Sin and Danger of Self-Love," in which Cushman had written off "beggary and gentry" as equally unwanted in the New World.[9]

[8]Benjamin Franklin, *The Writings of Benjamin Franklin*, ed. Albert Henry Smyth, 10 vols. (New York: Macmillan, 1905-07), 8: 603-14; quotations from pp. 605, 613.

[9]Franklin differed from the physiocrats more than he agreed with them. According to Alfred Owen Aldridge, they saw "America as a paradise of prosperity without arduous individual labor." The *Information for Those Who Would Remove to America*, adds Aldridge, "was written in part to counteract such rapturous impressions as this one." See *Franklin and his French Contemporaries* (New York: New York University Press, 1957), p. 30. Franklin's stress on frugality and economic independence was more compatible with the assumptions of the so-called Commonwealthmen or radical Whigs, a group of eighteenth-century English intellectuals whose writings helped to inspire the American Revolution. The similarity between Puritan and Whig social ideas is discussed by Gordon S. Wood in *The Creation of the American Republic, 1776-1787* (Chapel Hill: University of North Carolina Press, 1969), pp. 53-70, 114-18. The view that Americans were predominantly middle-class in the latter half

Franklin's secular appeal to those with middle-class aspirations did not make him contemptuous of the competing efforts of organized religion to foster the bourgeois virtues. Insofar as conventional creeds served to stimulate civic responsibility and to inculate the Puritan social ethic—his devout father, after all, had cherished that ethic too—he approved of them and contributed to the support of their ministers. He even continued his annual subscription to the Presbyterian congregation of the Reverand Mr. Andrews, and he maintained a sincere if "mere civil Friendship" with George Whitefield until the minister's death (p. 178). He could no more accept Whitefield's theology than his father's, and he rebuffed the former's periodic attempts to convert him. Yet he did not hesitate to give the great preacher his due. He was impressed and personally stirred by Whitefield's efficacy as an orator, as shown by the famous experiment in which he calculated that the evangelist's stentorian voice had the range to be heard by "25000 People in the Fields" (p. 179). Since his own *Almanack,* as he remarks in the *Autobiography,* sold ten thousand copies annually, Whitefield's words ostensibly reached the larger audience. In view of the minister's overpowering delivery, he might have been expected to generate an unrivaled force for good.

Yet Franklin did not regard George Whitefield as an altogether successful figure. The religious enthusiasm he kindled during his infrequent visits to Philadelphia apparently had a way of waning after his departures; by 1749, according to Franklin, the fervor Whitefield had aroused in 1740 had "long since abated" (p. 194). Whitefield's powers were simply too tied to his own physical presence to result in lasting benefits. Moreover, the brilliance of his oratory was not duplicated in his printed sermons. Filled with erroneous facts and unguarded opinions, they exposed him to violent sectarian criticism and ultimately decreased the number of his followers. *"Litera scripta manet,"* Franklin tersely observes: the written word endures, and in the

---

of the eighteenth century has been called into question by numerous demographic studies. It should be pointed out, however, that Franklin was articulating an ideology—an ideology whose appeal may have derived from its insistence on American uniqueness and middle-class homogeneity at the very period when America was ceasing to be either socially homogeneous or particularly unique in comparison to Europe.

case of Whitefield it endured to his permanent discredit (p. 180). In reading such a passage, we are apt to think of Franklin's own success as a writer and propagandist, to which he called repeated attention. Though Franklin also committed errata, he was flexible enough to confess and correct them; the zealous Whitefield's published mistakes were the cause of his decline.

Franklin's prudence thus proved a more effective means of advancing the social welfare than the evangelist's piety. While revivalists and other clergymen were busy spreading religion, and often embroiling themselves in disputes over doctrinal niceties, Franklin was hard at work disseminating his secular gospel and bettering the lives of his countrymen—spreading citizenship and progress, as it were. In these endeavors he had no peer in the colonies, and much of part three is taken up with listing his now familiar contributions in the area of "public Affairs" (p. 173). Even ministers had occasion to profit from his expertise. The Reverend Gilbert Tennent, second only to Edwards among native American "awakeners," appealed to Franklin for advice in the technique of fundraising. He applied Franklin's shrewd counsel with such success that "he obtain'd a much larger sum than he expected" for the construction of the Second Presbyterian Church (p. 202). The clergy obviously had more to learn from Franklin than to teach him, and their own experiences only testified to the superiority of his utilitarian ethic. Franklin himself emerges from the *Autobiography* as the embodiment of what was most constructive in the native spirit.

With the completion of part three, however, there arose a serious difficulty for Franklin—a difficulty which cannot simply be brushed aside with the explanation that the author was now an old man, past eighty, and unable to continue with his memoirs because of the infirmities of age. He terminated this section with the flat sentence, "We arrived in London the 27th of July 1757" (p. 259), and England, the scene of the worst of his youthful errata, had witnessed their recrudescence. Shortly after his arrival in London, for example, he had taken up residence with Mrs. Margaret Stevenson, who remained his mistress for some eighteen years. He also had sought out and resumed his friendship with James Ralph, and cooperated with Ralph's wish to conceal his first marriage from his present wife. In England, then, and later in France, Franklin had systematically if privately betrayed the social and moral philosophy he was propounding in the *Auto-biography*. Doubtless for this reason the brief fourth installment, which he composed during the winter of 1789-1790, carries the narrative only into the following year and casts him entirely in the role of a public figure, with no glimpse at all into his personal life. The outline in which he projected the remainder of the book consists primarily of a dry, staccato recitation of political events: "Congress, Assembly. Committee of Safety. Chevaux de Frize. Sent to Boston, to the Camp. To Canada. to Lord Howe. To France, Treaty, &c." (p. 272). Nowhere are Franklin's ideological motives cast into bolder relief than in this monotonous catalogue. He could not go into detail about his life abroad without betraying his personal recidivism, and to do so, of course, would have been to defeat his very purpose in writing.

The last year covered in the *Autobiography,* 1758, was also the year in which Franklin published *The Way to Wealth.* The coincidence is appropriate because the piece is a clever attack on the Calvinist clergy. It features "a plain, clean old Man" called Father Abraham who advocates at interminable length Franklin's own gospel of industry and thrift. Franklin was not making light of his teachings, however, so much as the drab method of their exposition. By putting them in the mouth of an Old Testament figure whose delivery rendered them useless, he was saying in effect that even the best of precepts could be made unpalatable if they were preached rather than taught by example. Indeed, no sooner has Father Abraham finished his discourse than his hearers proceed to practice "the contrary, just as if it had been a common Sermon."[10]

But there was a serious intent beneath the satirical surface of Franklin's "sermon," and a calculated reason for his choice of Father Abraham as the spokesman for his utilitarian ethic. In the Old Testament, God covenanted with Abraham as the father of Israel, and Americans of Franklin's day regarded themselves as the descendants of the biblical Hebrews. As the new chosen people, they believed they were destined to establish a paradise on earth. Franklin was telling his countrymen that it was not God but rather his maxims for achieving prosperity that had the pow-

[10]Franklin, *Papers,* 7: 340, 350.

er to transform America into the Promised Land. "If the Lord be with a people," Cotton Mather had stated a generation earlier, "they shall prosper in all their affairs." In Franklin's revision of the covenant, *"God helps them that help themselves."* Let us practice Poor Richard's virtues, he advised his readers, if we wish to prosper both individually and as a people.[11]

Not all Americans were ready, however, to accept Poor Richard's proverbs as a national orthodoxy. Franklin's harshest critics included the American romancers, and they had good reason to fear the spread of his ideas. Prizing progress above all else, he assumed the primacy of an economic individualism which devalued all "other modes of thought, feeling and action"[12] — including spiritual salvation, the joys of recreation, and artistic achievement. If the principle of delayed gratification, the crown of Franklin's system, built libraries and paved the streets, it also denied man's deepest needs. Its inevitable consequence was the faceless, dehumanized public servant of the last pages of the *Autobiography,* the Franklin whom Melville called "the type and genius of his land" and whose spirit still broods over America.

Despite the cosmopolitan elements of his thought, Franklin remained — in Carl Becker's words — "pungently American,"[13] and his greatest impact was upon America's social and cultural traditions. The famous scene of his entrance into Philadelphia is reminiscent of William Bradford's equally famous description of his arrival at Plymouth after the *Mayflower*'s stormy crossing to America. Both men paused in later life to call attention to the moment: Franklin, poor, dirty, and worn out from his journey, knowing no soul "nor where to look for Lodging," asked his readers to "compare such unlikely Beginnings with the Figure I have since made there" (p. 75). Bradford wrote that

> here I cannot but stay and make a pause, and stand half amazed at this poor people's present condition; and so I think will the reader, too, when he well considers the same. Being thus passed the vast ocean, and a sea of troubles before in their preparation...they had

[11] Mather, *The Way to Prosperity* (1690), in *The Wall and the Garden: Selected Massachusetts Election Sermons, 1670-1775,* ed. A. W. Plumstead (Minneapolis: University of Minnesota Press, 1968), p. 124; Franklin, *Papers,* 7: 341.

[12] The phrase is used by Ian Watt in *The Rise of the Novel* (Berkeley: University of California Press, 1957), p. 64.

[13] *Dictionary of American Biography,* s.v. "Benjamin Franklin."

now no friends to welcome them nor inns to entertain or refresh
their weatherbeaten bodies; no houses nor much less towns to repair to, to seek for succour.

Where could these weary pilgrims turn for sustenance, Bradford
cried, but to "the Spirit of God and His Grace"? Franklin emphasized the contrast between his humble origins and his present
eminence in order to dramatize his material ascent and dazzle
the youth of "a *rising* people" with the utility of his acquisitive
ethic; Bradford, praising the Lord for his mercies to a generation
in adversity, implored "the children of these fathers" to remember Him for "His loving kindness and His wonderful works before the sons of men."[14] The difference in their appeals brings
starkly into focus the displacement of a vision of piety and prudence by a narrowed creed of prudence alone. Franklin himself
made this point in *The Way to Wealth* when he struck off an
aphorism which recapitulates the whole of his philosophy: *"In
the Affairs of this World,"* he had Father Abraham say, para-
phrasing from the *Almanack, "Men are saved, not by Faith, but
by the Want of it."*[15]

[In the "Introduction" to his book, Gilmore argues that the
great writers of the American Renaissance developed out of "the
middle way"—between antinomianism and Arminianism—of the
Calvinist tradition. This inevitably caused them to react sharply
against Franklin. These concluding remarks illustrate a representative reaction on the part of Melville. Ed.]

The existential dilemmas which seem to confront so many
American characters are independent of economic, social, and
political issues. And yet these issues have a crucial importance
in our imaginative literature. American writers have been deeply
engaged by a conflict of values which stems from the dominance
in this country—or so our writers have often felt—of an ideology
that threatens the survival of art. It is an ideology that enthrones
material progress at the expense of spiritual aspirations, and for
many American authors it is symbolized, if only obliquely, by the

---

[14]William Bradford, *Of Plymouth Plantation,* ed. Samuel Eliot Morison (New
York: Alfred A. Knopf, 1952), pp. 61-63.
[15]Franklin, *Papers,* 7: 344.

person of Benjamin Franklin. Like countless other students of our history, they saw Franklin as a landmark in the secularization and corruption of the Puritan mind, a leading exponent of the "bourgeois heresy" that worldly success is the means or sign of redemption. They were critical of him and others like him for substituting prudence, moderation and the competitive ethic for religious imperatives and beliefs.[16]

One brief illustration, drawn from the turbulent decade before the Civil War, may give some idea of the literary response to the values associated with Franklin. It may also serve as an introduction to the concerns that will command our attention in the following pages. The example is Melville's "Lightning-Rod Man," which originally appeared in *Harper's* in 1854.[17] It has often been noticed that Melville's story shows the influence of the *Magnalia Christi Americana*, reprinted the year before, and the indebtedness yields a clue to its underlying theme: the nostrum peddled by the title character in the name of religion perverts the faith of a Puritan like Mather. It is quite to the point that the stranger deals in mechanical safety devices to protect men from the "supernal bolt." Melville surely expects the reader to remember that Franklin invented the lightning rod.

The salesman is Melville's reminder that Franklin's ideas are a fundamental component of American thought. He preaches a doctrine of salvation by prudence, imploring the narrator—a mountaineer and "lover of the majestic"—to quit his hearth and stand in "the exact middle of the cottage." We learn in the course

[16]A word of caution is in order in generalizing about what Americans thought or believed. We have learned, for example, a good deal about the social and economic views of the Puritan leaders. But our information is only fragmentary when it comes to their followers, the ordinary inhabitants of the New England colonies. We are almost as ignorant about the sentiments of the average citizen of the nineteenth century, who is quite inarticulate from the standpoint of history. When I speak of an American ideology, I am referring to the beliefs of specific individuals such as Franklin, and I do not wish to make the claim that the convictions or impressions of a few necessarily reflect the attitudes of the populace at large. What can be said with some certainty is that our greatest writers have voiced their opposition to a system of values whose prevalence in America has been remarked on by critics and advocates alike. They have challenged those values from a world view rooted in essentially Calvinist premises.

[17]The story is reprinted in Herman Melville, *The Complete Stories of Herman Melville*, ed. Jay Leyda (New York: Random House, 1949), pp. 213-21.

of the story, however, that the stranger's rods and precautions are inimical to the spirit of authentic religion and jeopardize its very existence. The steeple of a nearby church, equipped with one of his devices, has only the week before been destroyed by lightning, and he himself takes particular care never to touch iron in the midst of a thunder storm, not excluding bells in belfries. He says that he makes it his business to shun crowds and especially tall men, at which the horrified narrator blurts out, "Do I dream? Man avoid man? and in danger-time, too?" Exclaiming *"Mine* is the only true rod," he thrice commands the narrator, "Come hither to me!"—to the safety of the middle of the room. But the mountaineer, drawing himself up as erect as he can, refuses to budge from his hearthstone. Thus does Melville, who trusts that "the Deity will not, of purpose, make war on man's earth," hurl his denial at the satanic tempters of his day, an act of resistance which provokes the frustrated salesman to denounce him as an "impious wretch."

Melville and writers like him were indeed irreverent in their hostility toward an ideology which they feared was becoming a national faith. The pun on "rod," in the salesman's exclamation, and the final disclosure that the stranger still dwells in the land, driving "a brave trade with the fears of man," vividly convey Melville's deep disquiet over the state of America as the Civil War neared. The rod of an angry God was poised to descend upon a people who had forsaken their principles by countenancing slavery and deserting Protestantism for the Protestant ethic. It is not by chance that *The Confidence-Man,* published three years later, ends with an apocalyptic vision in which an old man, presumably Uncle Sam, is escorted into the metaphorical darkness of hell. The hopes that sped the *Arbella* in 1630 perished for Melville aboard the *Fidèle.*

The Dogood Letters

by Kenneth S. Lynn

The first of the series of letters which Franklin contributed to the *New-England Courant* under the *nom de plume* of Silence Dogood appeared in the issue of April 2, 1722. Published by Franklin's older brother, the *Courant* spoke for those Anglicans and deists (and possibly some Puritan saints as well) who longed for the sophisticated tone of London life. James Franklin's newspaper gave them a reasonable facsimile, in the form of imitations of Sir Roger de Coverley. Letters to the editor from local wits who signed themselves Tabitha Talkative, Ichabod Henroost, Fanny Mournful (or Silence Dogood) satirized Bostonian foibles in what they dearly hoped was the true *Tatler* or *Spectator* manner. The fun seemed harmless, especially since James Franklin promised not to print anything that would reflect on the clergy, but in fact it was dynamite.

As Bergson points out, comedy stands midway between life and the "disinterestedness" of most art in that it "accepts social life as a natural environment" and even has a "scarcely conscious intention to correct and instruct." Just as the *Tatler's* announced purpose was to expose the "false arts of life," so the provincial imitator had, as Benjamin Franklin confessed in the *Courant's* pages, "a natural inclination to observe and reprove the faults of others." In the Boston of the 1720s, however, the role of social corrector and instructor was still very much the prerogative of the ministry, and the Mathers were not the kind of Christians who surrendered prerogatives without a fight. When in its early issues the *Courant* ridiculed the Mather-supported idea that inoculation for smallpox might halt the epidemic that was sweeping Boston, it thereby furnished Cotton Mather with an excuse for meeting the threat to his position head on: "The practice of supporting and publishing every week a libel on purpose to lessen and blacken and burlesque the virtuous and principal ministers of religion in a country, and render the services of their ministry despicable, even detestable, to the people, is a wickedness that was never known before in any country, Christian, Turkish or Pagan, on the face of the earth." The battle was protracted, but the outcome was inevitable. In June of 1722 James Franklin was jailed for three weeks for contempt of the government; the following January he was accused of mocking religion and forbidden to publish his newspaper except under the supervision of the Secretary of the Province. It was at this point that the indentured younger brother became the ostensible publisher, but the subterfuge was short-lived. In September of 1723 the *Courant* advertised for a "likely lad for an apprentice"—the younger Franklin, it seems, had run off to seek his fortune. Not quite three years later the *Courant* folded.

But if the Mathers thus held onto their prerogative, they were nevertheless powerless to exercise it effectively. In the second volume of *The New England Mind,* Professor Perry Miller has demonstrated that by the end of the first quarter of the eighteenth century Boston was a very different society from what it had been fifty years before, and that the ministerial leadership had lost contact with the reality of the new age. Certainly this was Franklin's view of the situation. In Number IV of the Dogood letters, he suggested that Harvard College, the great training ground of the ministry, was producing only conceited blockheads, and in Number IX he wondered why it was that moral hypocrites could easily deceive the ministers long after the people had seen through their masquerade. For a moralist, such ignorance on the part of the learned leaders of society constituted an intolerable state of affairs, and even at sixteen years of age Franklin was a moralist. All his thinking life he adhered to the belief of his youth that "the happiness or real good of men consists in right action, and right action cannot be produced without right opinion

...[therefore] it behoves us, above all things in this world, to take care that our opinions of things be according to the nature of things." But those who were officially charged with this care no longer understood the nature of things, and so in the spring of 1722 Benjamin Franklin slipped the first of the Dogood letters under the door of his brother's printing house.

The letters make evident a cheerful affection for improper Bostonians; Franklin knew, as the author of *Pamela* did not, that "to be proud of one's virtue is like poisoning one's self with the antidote." But it was precisely because he knew raffish Boston so well that he could be quite clear in his mind that "the good of man is not natural and sensual, but rational and moral," and the comedy of the Dogood letters is always directed toward that revelation. Franklin's genial cynicism conceals the high serious-ness of a moral teacher. The sharp edge of the humor in this early work is occasionally blunted by amateurish writing, but Boston would have to wait for Jonathan Edwards to come out of the Connecticut Valley before religion would regain its power to instruct the community with a greater effectiveness than Silence Dogood's.

What is most significant about this story of the Dogood letters is that it reveals the relationship of American humor to American religion. The invention of Silence Dogood filled a moral vacuum created by the blindness of the clergy; in a period of religious declension, the humorist took over from the minister. This was the first time in American history that such a thing had hap-pened, but it was not the last. Franklin is not the only American humorist who was a minister *manqué,* a Puritan in reverse, whose humor was at once irreverent and more serious than the churches. At the heart of the laughter of Mark Twain, Ring Lardner, and Sinclair Lewis, there is a raging Puritanical didacticism that few contemporary sermons could match.

The style of the Dogood letters reveals the relation of Franklin's humor to religion in another way. The letters were consciously modeled on Addison, whom Franklin greatly admired. But whereas Addison's prose is, in the words of Dr. Johnson, "the model of the middle style...always equable, and always easy," Franklin's style constantly sacrifices urbanity for the sake of the homely, specific image or the vivid detail. Franklin tried to imitate the polish of Addison, but he could not escape the fact that he had been raised on the earthiness of Bunyan. As a humorist Franklin was a secular priest, and Silence Dogood speaks in a voice that mixes the accents of the *Spectator* papers and *Pilgrim's Progress*.

The Almanac

by Bruce Granger

On December 28, 1732, the *Pennsylvania Gazette* announced
as "JUST PUBLISHED, FOR 1733,"

> POOR RICHARD: An ALMANACK containing the Lunations, Eclipses,
> Planets Motions and Aspects, Weather, Sun and Moon's rising and
> setting, Highwater, &c. besides many pleasant and witty Verses,
> Jests and Sayings, Author's Motive of Writing, Prediction of the
> Death of his friend Mr. Titan Leeds, Moon no Cuckold, Batchelor's
> Folly, Parson's Wine and Baker's Pudding, Short Visits, Kings and
> Bears, New Fashions, Game for Kisses, Katherine's Love, Dif-
> ferent Sentiments, Signs of a Tempest, Death of Fisherman, Con-
> jugal Debate, Men and Melons, H. the Prodigal, Breakfast in Bed,
> Oyster Lawsuit, &c. by RICHARD SAUNDERS, Philomat.

Poor Richard's Almanack was by no means the first such production in Pennsylvania, where farmers, artisans, and shopkeepers
demanded a literature of action. As early as 1686 Samuel Atkins
had tried his hand at the form, and Daniel Leeds took his place
the next year.[1] From the turn of the century the colony witnessed a steady flow of almanacs. When Franklin undertook his,
no fewer than six others were being published at Philadelphia,
several of them written and printed by men like Andrew Bradford, Samuel Keimer, and Thomas Godfrey whom he knew
personally.

"The Almanac." From *Benjamin Franklin: An American Man of Letters,*
by Bruce Granger. Copyright 1964 by Cornell University Press. Reprinted
through the courtesy of Bruce Ingham Granger. The chapter has been slightly
abridged by the present editor.

[1] John Bach McMaster, *Benjamin Franklin as a Man of Letters* (Boston and
New York, 1887), p. 99.

In his almanacs Franklin, the rising young editor, wrote with greater familiarity than he allowed himself in his more studied periodical essays; after all, as philomath he did not need to maintain the same dignity as in the *Gazette.* Considering *Poor Richard* "a proper Vehicle for conveying Instruction among the common People, who bought scarce any other Books," he "endeavour'd to make it both entertaining and useful."[2] He approached his task in seeming earnest, thereby escaping the prosaic dullness that characterized most colonial almanacs. In 1737 "Philomath," expressing what was certainly Franklin's attitude, specified "the Talents requisite in *an Almanack Writer.*" Contending that *"Almanackorum scriptor nascitur non fit,"* he said that such a writer *"should be descended of a great Family, and bear a Coat of Arms";* that he should possess "a Sort of Gravity, which keeps a due medium between Dulness and Nonsense, and yet has a Mixture of both.... He shou'd write Sentences, and throw out Hints, that neither himself, nor any Body else can understand or know the meaning of"; and that he *"shou'd not be a finish'd Poet, but a Piece of one,* and qualify'd to write, what we vulgarly call Doggerel." "I could further prove to you, if I was to go about it," concluded Philomath, "That an *Almanack Writer* ought not only to be a Piece of a Wit, but a very Wag; and that he shou'd have the Art also to make People believe, that he is almost a Conjurer, &c."[3]

I

In the prefaces to *Poor Richard's Almanack* and occasionally in the verse Franklin created his most famous American personae, the homespun Richard Saunders and his clacking wife Bridget. "I might in this place attempt to gain thy Favour," Richard informs the reader in the first number,

> by declaring that I write Almanacks with no other View than that of the publick Good; but in this I should not be sincere; and Men are now a-days too wise to be deceiv'd by Pretences how specious soever. The plain Truth of the Matter is, I am excessive poor, and

[2]*Benjamin Franklin's Memoirs. Parallel Text Edition,* ed. Max Farrand (Berkeley and Los Angeles, 1949), p. 242.
[3]*Pennsylvania Gazette,* October 20, 1737.

my Wife, good Woman, is, I tell her, excessive proud; she cannot
bear, she says, to sit spinning in her Shift of Tow, while I do nothing
but gaze at the Stars; and has threatned more than once to burn all
my Books and Rattling-Traps (as she calls my Instruments) if I do
not make some profitable Use of them for the good of my Family.
The Printer has offer'd me some considerable share of the Profits,
and I have thus begun to comply with my Dame's desire.[4]

His first almanac sells so well that at once he gains a measure of
relief: "My Wife has been enabled to get a Pot of her own, and is
no longer oblig'd to borrow one from a Neighbour; nor have we
ever since been without something of our own to put in it. She
has also got a pair of Shoes, two new Shifts, and a new warm Petticoat; and for my part, I have bought a second-hand Coat, so good,
that I am now not asham'd to go to Town or be seen there. These
Things have render'd her Temper so much more pacifick than
it us'd to be, that I may say, I have slept more, and more quietly
within this last Year, than in the three foregoing Years put
together" (1734). A prospering Richard assures his readers, "If
the generous Purchaser of my Labours could see how often his
Fi'-pence helps to light up the comfortable Fire, line the Pot,
fill the Cup and make glad the Heart of a poor Man and an honest
good old Woman, he would not think his Money ill laid out,
tho' the Almanack of his Friend and Servant R. SAUNDERS were
one half blank Paper" (1737). Lest they suppose him grown
wealthy, though, he reminds them that the printer, though "I do
not grudge it him," "runs away with the greatest Part of the
Profit" (1739).

From the outset the *Almanack's* purpose was wholly social.
Like the Busy-Body, Richard professes and adheres to a neu-
trality in religion and politics. In 1746 he assures his public,

> Free from the bitter Rage of Party Zeal,
> All those we love who seek the publick Weal.

Indeed, other than his attacks on fellow philomaths like Titan
Leeds and John Jerman, attacks for which Swift's Bickerstaff
papers furnished a precedent, Franklin avoided polemics al-

---

[4]*The Papers of Benjamin Franklin,* ed. Leonard W. Labaree et al. (New
Haven: Yale University Press, 1959-), I, 311. Hereafter all quotations from
Poor Richard will be identified by year and month in the body of the text.

together, exhibiting instead that sweet reasonableness and moralistic bent so highly esteemed in the early eighteenth century.
As the Couranteers had entertained their readers with the age-
old battle of the sexes, so now Franklin. To Richard's charge,

> She that will eat her breakfast in her bed,
> And spend the morn in dressing of her head,
> And sit at dinner like a maiden bride,
> And talk of nothing all day but of pride;
> God in his mercy may do much to save her,
> But what a case is he in that shall have her.
>   [Dec., 1733]

Bridget retorts,

> He that for the sake of Drink neglects his Trade,
> And spends each Night in Taverns till 'tis late,
> And rises when the Sun is four hours high,
> And ne'er regards his starving Family;
> God in his Mercy may do much to save him,
> But, woe to the poor Wife, whose Lot it is to have him.
>   [Dec., 1734]

The lines of battle thus early drawn, Bridget cries out against
Richard's aspersions on her character: "What a peasecods!
cannot I have a little Fault or two, but all the Country must see
it in print! They have already been told, at one time that I am
proud, another time that I am loud, and that I have got a new
Petticoat, and abundance of such kind of stuff; and now, forsooth! all the World must know, that Poor Dick's Wife has lately
taken a fancy to drink a little Tea now and then. A mighty matter, truly, to make a Song of! 'Tis true, I had a little Tea of a
Present from the Printer last Year; and what, must a body throw
it away?" (1738). When placed side by side with Mrs. Afterwit,
Bridget seems the soul of modesty; in fact, her practicality,
honesty, and industry call to mind rather the Widow Dogood.
No matter, the battle raged on.

> My sickly Spouse, with many a Sigh
> Once told me,—Dicky I shall die:
> I griev'd, but recollected strait,
> 'Twas bootless to contend with Fate:
> So Resignation to Heav'n's Will

> Prepared me for succeeding Ill;
> 'Twas well it did; for, on my Life,
> 'Twas Heav'n's Will to spare my Wife.
> [Jan., 1740]

When he tells her that heaven will deny whatever she prays for, "Indeed! says Nell, 'tis what I'm pleas'd to hear;/ For now I'll pray for your long life, my dear" (Sept., 1743). Finally, in what closes out this debate, there appeared an *"Epitaph on a Scolding Wife by her Husband,"* adapted from Dryden: "Here my poor Bridget's Corps doth lie, she is at rest,—and so am I" (Dec., 1744).

Although Richard Saunders has often been confused with his creator, the separate identity of the humble philomath grown affluent and his printer was clearly established from the opening number. So it is that Richard, in order to quash malicious rumors that there is no such man as he and that his productions are actually the work of the printer, publicly declares, *"That what I have written heretofore, and do now write, neither was nor is written by any other Man or Men, Person or Persons whatsoever"* (1736). So, too, that he holds the printer, not himself, accountable for most of the errata in one of the almanacs, remarking:

> Printers indeed should be very careful how they omit a Figure or a Letter: For by such Means sometimes a terrible Alteration is made in the Sense. I have heard, that once, in a new Edition of the *Common Prayer,* the following Sentence, *We shall all be changed in a Moment, in the Twinkling of an Eye;* by the Omission of a single Letter, became, *We shall all be hanged in a Moment, &c.* to the no small Surprize of the first Congregation it was read to (1750).

This confusion between the author and his persona arises in part from the fact that after 1738 Richard the honest philomath tends to be obscured by the emergence of Richard the moralizing philosopher, a confusion later compounded by the avowedly didactic purpose of the often reprinted *Autobiography.* "Besides the usual Things expected in an Almanack," declares Richard in 1739, "I hope the profess'd Teachers of Mankind will excuse my scattering here and there some instructive Hints in Matters of Morality and Religion." From this time, but especially beginning in 1748, the year Franklin expanded his pamphlet from twenty-four pages to thirty-six, didactic and practical essays become more numerous and play a more prominent role in the *Almanack*.

Any final estimate of the character of Richard must take into account the 1758 Preface, known familiarly as *The Way to Wealth*, a work allied to popular tradesman books like Defoe's *Complete English Tradesman* and English conduct books like John Barnard's *Present for an Apprentice*. While Franklin's first object in living was to master the art of virtue and while he undoubtedly gave general assent to the wisdom of Poor Richard, here it is so narrowly concentrated and cast in so precise a narrative frame that Franklin probably did not mean the work to be taken altogether seriously.[5] But eighteenth-century France, identifying Franklin's attitude with Richard's, regarded it "as a work of sublime morality";[6] and since that time readers the world over have generally so interpreted it. Actually we see Richard, hearing himself quoted so liberally, enslaved by his own morality, a fact of which Franklin is clearly aware. Whereas the people at the auction, having approved the doctrine in Father Abraham's speech, "immediately practised the contrary, just as if it had been a common Sermon," Richard takes this prudential wisdom — and it is, of course, his own — so much to heart that he denies himself material for a new coat, even though the one he is wearing was secondhand when he bought it a quarter of a century before. And when he adds smugly, *"Reader, if thou wilt do the same, thy Profit will be as great as mine,"* though we do not necessarily sympathize with the behavior of the others "at this Vendue of *Fineries* and *Knicknacks,"* we smile at the foolish caution that prevents him from making a reasonable purchase. Franklin, who prized frugality as highly as any man, is here warning his public not to fall victim to a narrow and unimaginative exercise of it.[7]

At this point I should like to revise one judgment in John F.

[5] Alfred Owen Aldridge, *Franklin and His French Contemporaries* (New York, 1957), p. 53, writes, "That Franklin himself did not take it seriously, the narrative elements with which he adorned it are ample proof."

[6] Ibid., p. 59.

[7] Harold S. Larrabee, *Harper's Magazine*, CCXII (Jan., 1956), 66, says of Franklin, "His moral teaching — like that of John Dewey, now so much under attack — was a dynamic doctrine of 'open ends' rather than of fixed moral absolutes forcing all individuals into a single mold."

Ross's otherwise highly perceptive article on the character of Richard Saunders. Having distinguished carefully between the two Richards, Ross remarks:

> It is easy to see why Franklin let the original character go, and made no attempt to relate the maxims to the character of his star-gazer. He was interested in getting an almanac to press every fall, not in the depiction of character or the maintenance of literary consistency. ... The early Richard was finally submerged by the famous farewell preface of 1758, wherein a shadowy Richard appears, only to introduce the speech of a wise old man, Father Abraham, who quotes maxim after maxim from the body of the almanacs. ... That is, Franklin forced Richard to play a rôle.[8]

Granted that as Franklin built a comfortable living in the 1740's, he began to conceive of Richard as the complete American tradesman. Granted, too, that by the 1750's the *Almanack* was selling at the impressive rate of 10,000 copies a year.[9] I cannot accept the inference that he consciously forced Richard to play a role. It seems more probable that insofar as the conception of Richard underwent a change, it happened unconsciously. And if Franklin was not immediately concerned with maintaining literary consistency, how is it that the original Richard reappears in the 1750's—nowhere more memorably than in *The Way to Wealth,* where he is anything but "shadowy"? The enduring vitality of this, Franklin's most fully articulated persona, lies finally in the fact that over the space of twenty-five years the character of the indigent stargazer turned philomath is never totally submerged.

II

Balzac, in a statement that is true in spirit if not wholly in fact, once observed, *"Le canard est une trouvaille de Franklin, qui a inventé le paratonnerre, le canard et la république."*[10] The earliest of Franklin's canards, recalling Swift's hoax on John Partridge, was perpetrated at the expense of a local rival, Titan Leeds. The equation: Richard Saunders is to Titan Leeds as Isaac Bicker-

[8]*PMLA,* LV (1940), 793-94.
[9]C. William Miller, *Studies in Bibliography,* XIV (1961), 111.
[10]*Illusions perdues* (Paris, 1879), II, 115.

staff is to John Partridge: expresses the similarity in rhetorical strategy, though in certain respects Richard resembles Partridge more nearly than he does Bickerstaff. In the 1733 Preface Richard predicts the time of Titan's death to the minute and, when Titan protests that he did not die at that time, earnestly defends his prediction:

> Mr. Leeds was not only profoundly skillful in the useful Science he profess'd, but he was a Man of *exemplary Sobriety,* a most *sincere Friend,* and an *exact Performer of his Word.* These valuable Qualifications, with many others so much endear'd him to me, that although it should be so, that, contrary to all Probability, contrary to my Prediction and his own, he might possibly be yet alive, yet my Loss of Honour as a Prognosticator, cannot afford me so much Mortification, as his Life, Health and Safety would give me Joy and Satisfaction (1734).

Titan's protests continuing, Richard retorts with pretended indignation:

> Having receiv'd much Abuse from Titan Leeds deceas'd, (Titan Leeds when living would not have us'd me so!)... I cannot help saying, that tho' I take it patiently, I take it very unkindly. And whatever he may pretend, 'tis undoubtedly true that he is really defunct and dead. First because the Stars are seldom disappointed. ...Secondly,...for the Honour of Astrology, the Art professed both by him and his Father [Daniel] before him. Thirdly,...[because] his two last Almanacks...are not written with that *Life* his Performances use to be written with (1735).

In 1739, by Richard's account, the Bradfords, who continued to publish Titan's almanac, at last admit that he is dead. Whereupon Richard relates how, waking early one morning at his study table where he had fallen asleep, he discovered a letter from Titan confessing that he had indeed died at the time predicted, "with a Variation only of 5 min. 53 sec." Titan goes on to explain further:

> Finding you asleep, I entred your left Nostril, ascended into your Brain, found out where the Ends of those Nerves were fastned that move your right Hand and Fingers, by the Help of which I am now writing unknown to you; but when you open your Eyes, you will see that the Hand written is mine, tho' wrote with yours (1740).

Here for the first time Franklin employs a rhetorical strategy that colored later writings like Polly Baker's Speech and the fictitious controversy involving English news writers. He initiates, carries forward, and closes out this hoax, not through malice, but for the pleasure to be gained from exploiting the comic implications of the fiction. Once Richard has predicted the time of Titan's death, pseudological proofs follow hard upon one another, the principal strategy being to seize upon the victim's every protest of innocence and turn it back upon him. Thus, in reply to Titan's declaration, "Saunders adds another GROSS FALSHOOD in his Almanack, viz. that by my own Calculation I shall *survive* until the 26th of the said Month October 1733, which is as *untrue* as the former," Richard asserts, "Now if it be, as Leeds says, *untrue* and a *gross Falshood* that he surviv'd till the 26th of October 1733, then it is certainly *true* that he died *before* that Time" (1735). The climactic letter in which Titan admits to having died at the time predicted, "with a Variation only of 5 min, 53 sec.," bears final witness to Franklin's high sense of invention. This Swiftian hoax is part of a continuing, good-humored attack on astrology in the pages of the *Almanack*. Not so incidentally, the sophistry Richard here displays lends subtlety to his character.

Franklin, who took himself less seriously than did his rival philomaths, has Richard declare:

> The noble Art [of astrology] is dwindled into Contempt; the Great neglect us, Empires make Leagues, and Parliaments Laws, without advising with us; and scarce any other Use is made of our learned Labours, than to find the best Time of cutting Corns, or gelding Pigs. This Mischief we owe in a great Measure to ourselves. ... Urania has been betray'd by her own Sons; those whom she had favour'd with the greatest Skill in her divine Art, the most eminent Astronomers among the Moderns, the Newtons, Halleys, and Whistons, have wantonly contemn'd and abus'd her, contrary to the Light of their own Consciences (1751).

In the prefaces and essays such astrological lore as eclipses, weather predictions, and prophecies is constantly being held up to ridicule. Thus, Richard predicts two eclipses of the sun, "both, like Mrs. —s's Modesty, and old Neighbour Scrape-all's Money,

Invisible" (1734); and says of John Jerman's prediction, "He has done what in him lay (by sending them out to gaze at an invisible Eclipse on the first of April) to make *April Fools* of them all" (1744).

As for the weather, Richard asks that philomaths be allowed a few days' leeway, and, "if it does not come to pass accordingly, let the Fault be laid upon the Printer, who, 'tis very like, may have transpos'd or misplac'd it, perhaps for the Conveniency of putting in his Holidays" (1737). The year Bridget tampered with the almanac during her husband's absence she informs the reader, "Upon looking over the Months, I see he has put in abundance of foul Weather this Year; and therefore I have scatter'd here and there, where I could find room, some *fair, pleasant, sunshiny,* &c. for the Good-Women to dry their Clothes in" (1738). All in all, Richard is pleased to think that his weather predictions come to pass *"punctually* and *precisely* on the very Day, in some Place or other on this little *diminutive* Globe of ours" (1753).

Richard's "True PROGNOSTICATION, for 1739" is a skillful abstracting of the "Pantagruelian Prognostication" at the end of the Urquhart-Motteux translation of *Gargantua and Pantagruel,* with vernacular additions and substitutions made out of regard for an American audience. In a passage taken almost verbatim from Rabelais, Richard predicts: "During the first visible Eclipse Saturn is retrograde: For which Reason the Crabs will go sidelong, and the Ropemakers backward. The Belly will wag before, and the A--- shall sit down first." The passage continues: "Mercury will have his share in these Affairs, and so confound the Speech of People, that when a Pensilvanian would say PANTHER, he shall say PAINTER. When a New-Yorker thinks to say (THIS) he shall say (DISS) and the People in New England and Cape-May will not be able to say (COW) for their lives, but will be forc'd to say (KEOW) by a certain involuntary Twist in the Root of their Tongues." To Rabelais' prediction, "This Year the Stone-blind shall see but very little; the Deaf shall hear but poorly; and the Dumb shan't speak very plain," Richard adds, "And it's much, if my Dame Bridget talks at all this Year." For Rabelais' "Salt-eel" he substitutes the more homely expression "Cowskin"; for "Apes, Monkeys, Baboons, and Dromedaries," the more familiar "Cats, Dogs and Horses"; for "your Hops of Picardy," **the more** nearly American "Orange Trees in Greenland"; and for "Wine" and "Herbs," the less exotic "Cyder" and "Turnips." In this burlesque Franklin exhibits skill in compressing and adapting a literary source to his own very different purpose.

III

In addition to prefaces and essays, colonial almanacs traditionally carried what Franklin advertised as "pleasant and witty Verses, Jests and Sayings," that is, proverbial matter and poetic borrowings. B. J. Whiting has defined the proverb as "an expression which, owing its birth to the people, testifies to its origin in form and phrase. It expresses what is apparently a fundamental truth...in homely language, often adorned, however, with alliteration and rhyme; it is usually true, but need not be."[11] Judging by Swift's *Complete Collection of Genteel and Ingenious Conversation,* two dialogues burlesquing proverbial expressions of the day, and by Lord Chesterfield's admonition that his son avoid "old sayings, and common proverbs; which are so many proofs of having kept bad and low company,"[12] it seems safe to accept Robert Newcomb's assertion that during the first part of the eighteenth century "the educated Englishman's attitude toward the proverb was not very favorable."[13] As an artisan's son Franklin had no such reservations, however; from the time Silence Dogood announced that *"a Woman's Work is never done,"* proverbial expression was an essential component of his style.

Franklin filled the little spaces of his almanacs with what Richard calls *"moral* Sentences, *prudent* Maxims, and *wise* Sayings, many of them containing *much good Sense* in *very few* Words, and therefore apt to leave *strong* and *lasting* Impressions on the Memory of young Persons" (1747). These proverbs were gleaned principally from Thomas Fuller's *Gnomologia* (1732), *Introductio ad Prudentiam* (1727), and *Introductio ad Sapientiam*

[11]*Harvard Studies and Notes in Philology,* XIV (1932), 302.

[12]July 25, 1741, *The Letters of Philip Dormer Stanhope, 4th Earl of Chesterfield,* ed. Bonamy Dobree (London, 1932), II, 461.

[13]Robert Howard Newcomb, "The Sources of Benjamin Franklin's Sayings of Poor Richard" (unpublished dissertation, University of Maryland, 1957), p. 46.

(1731); Lord Halifax's *Character of King Charles the Second: and Political, Moral, Miscellaneous Thoughts and Reflections* (1750); George Herbert's *Outlandish Proverbs* (1640); James Howell's *Lexicon Tetraglotton* (1659); and Samuel Richardson's *Collection of Moral and Instructive Sentiments* (1755).[14] Such sayings, especially those that appear in the early numbers of the *Almanack,* usually reflect Richard's interests.[15]

While most of Richard's comic sayings are given verbatim from the original source, on occasion Franklin, yielding to a coarseness that was native to him, modifies them in the direction of the obscene or bawdy.

> A good friend is my nearest relation. [Fuller, *Gn.*, No. 151]
> Relation without friendship, friendship without power, power without will, will without effect, effect without profit, and profit without vertue, are not worth a farto.
> [*Poor Richard's Almanack*, Apr., 1733]
>
> A Fort which begins to parley is half gotten. [Howell, *It. Prov.*, p. 12]
> The Woman who hearkens, and the town which treats, the one will yield, the other will do. [Howell, *Fr. Prov.*, p. 5]
> Neither a Fortress nor a Maidenhead will hold out long after they begin to parly. [*PRA*, May, 1734]

The pun, a recognizable feature in the proverb, is so habitual to Franklin that he will introduce one where none is present in the original.

> The good wife is made by the man. [Howell, *Sp. Prov.*, p. 14]
> Good wives and good plantations are made by good husbands. [*PRA*, Aug., 1736]

The comic element present in such sayings further vivifies Franklin's most vital comic creation and goes far toward counteracting the stereotype of Richard the prudential moralist that persisted throughout the "inner-directed" nineteenth century and still lingers today.

[14]Newcomb has uncovered most of the sources for the sayings in *Poor Richard.* For his discussion of Franklin's borrowings from Halifax, Montaigne, and Richardson, see *PMLA*, LXX (1955), 535-39; Mod. Lang. Notes, LXXII (1957), 489-91; and Jour. Eng. and Germ. Phil., LVII (1958), 27-35.

[15]Newcomb, "Sources," p. 31.

As a proverb stylist who often recast what he borrowed, Franklin was guided by such neoclassic ideals as perspicuity, elegance, and cadence. In accommodating foreign sayings to an American audience, he habitually familiarizes and simplifies the diction.

> Nor wife, nor wine, nor horse ought to be praised. [Howell, *It. Prov.*, p. 12]
> Never praise your Cyder, Horse, or Bedfellow. [*PRA*, Mar., 1736]

> A yeoman upon his legs is higher than a prince upon his knees. [Fuller, *Gn.*, No. 488]
> A Plowman on his Legs is higher than a Gentleman on his Knees. [*PRA*, May, 1746]

> Go neither to the Physician upon every distemper, nor to the Lawyer upon every brabble, nor to the pot upon every thirst. [Howell, *Sp. Prov.*, p. 7]
> Don't go to the doctor with every distemper, nor to the lawyer with every quarrel, nor to the pot for every thirst. [*PRA*, Nov., 1737]

He tightens the syntax of many sayings and expresses the meaning in a narrower compass, sometimes employing alliteration or rhyme.

> That cheese is wholesomest which comes from a Miser. [Howell, *Sp. Prov.*, p. 23]
> The misers cheese is wholesomest. [*PRA*, Feb., 1737]

> As soon as men have understanding enough to find a fault, they have enough to see the danger of mending it. [Halifax, *Misc.*, p. 244]
> Men take more pains to mask than mend. [*PRA*, Apr., 1757]

> A ship under sail, a man in complete armor, a woman with a great belly are three of the handsomest sights. [Howell, *Eng. Prov.*, p. 2]
> A ship under sail and a big-bellied Woman,
> Are the handsomest two things that can be seen common. [*PRA*, June, 1735]

But since Franklin does not believe in economy for its own sake, he may see fit to expand the original saying. Such expansion is usually the result of supplying the saying with an introduction (often a personification), clarifying its sense by extending it, or appending a moral close.

He is a greater Liar than an epitaph. [Howell, *It. Prov.*, p. 2]
Here comes Glib-tongue: who can out-flatter a Dedication; and lie, like ten Epitaphs. [*PRA*, Dec., 1742]

Happy those who are convinced so as to be of the general opinions. [Halifax, *Polit.*, p. 227]
Singularity in the right, hath ruined many: Happy those who are Convinced of the general Opinion. [*PRA*, Oct., 1757]

A quiet Conscience sleeps in Thunder. [Fuller, *Gn.*, No. 375]
A quiet Conscience sleeps in Thunder,
But Rest and Guilt live far asunder. [*PRA*, July, 1747]

When all sins grow old covetousness grows young. [Herbert, No. 18]
When other Sins grow old by Time,
Then Avarice is in its prime,
Yet feed the Poor at Christmas time. [*PRA*, Dec., 1757]

To secure precision he modifies sayings in the direction of concreteness.

The tongue talks at the head's cost. [Herbert, p. 308]
The Tongue offends, and the Ears get the Cuffing, [*PRA*, Nov., 1757]

Slander would not stick, if it had not always something to lay hold of. [Halifax, *Misc.*, p. 255]
Act uprightly, and despise Calumny; Dirt may stick to a Mud Wall, but not to polish'd Marble. [*PRA*, Sept., 1757]

Revisions like these all make for greater perspicuity.

Such ornament as Richard's sayings possess is consistent with the responsible use of rhetoric enjoined by the Port-Royalists and Locke. Franklin at times introduces a metaphor into an original saying, at others amplifies or gives greater precision and consistency to one already present.

Nothing can be humbler than Ambition, when it is so disposed. [Halifax, *Moral*, p. 232]
Nothing humbler than *Ambition*, when it is about to climb. [*PRA*, Nov., 1753]

Who riseth late, trots all day, because he is behind hand with business. [Howell, *Sp. Prov.*, p. 27]
He that riseth late, must trot all day, and shall scarce overtake his business at night. [*PRA*, Aug., 1742]

That which is given shines, that which is eaten stinks. [Howell, *Fr. Prov.*, p. 8]
> What's given shines,
> What's receiv'd is rusty. [*PRA*, July, 1735]

Sometimes he supplies an example to point up and color a saying.

Necessity has no law. [Howell, *Eng. Prov.*, p. 9]
> *Necessity* has no Law; I know some Attorneys of the name. [*PRA*, Oct., 1734]

However elegantly Franklin dresses up Richard's sayings, he carefully avoids making a show of rhetoric.

Cadence, which John Hughes defined as "a Disposing of the Words in such Order, and with such Variation of Periods, as may strike the Ear with a sort of musical Delight," is markedly present in the sayings Franklin recasts. Frequently he strives for a more balanced expression, or one that is less mechanically balanced.

It is better to have an egg today than an hen tomorrow. [Howell, *It. Prov.*, p. 1]
> An Egg today is better than a Hen to-morrow. [*PRA*, Sept., 1734]

Thou shouldst grace thy House; not thy House thee. [Fuller, *Prud.*, No. 1796]
> Grace then thy House, and let not that grace thee. [*PRA*, Apr., 1739]

A Man had as good go to Bed to a Razor, as to be intimate with a foolish friend. [Halifax, *Moral*, p. 235]
> To be intimate with a foolish Friend, is like going to bed to a Razor. [*PRA*, Sept., 1754]

When one Knave betrayeth another, the one is not to be blamed, nor the other to be pitied. [Halifax, *Moral*, p. 237]
> When Knaves betray each other, one can scarce be blamed, or the other pitied. [*PRA*, Feb., 1758]

To strengthen the rhythm of the sentence he often* employs alliteration.

A Melon and a woman are hard to be known. [Howell, *Sp. Prov.*, p. 4]
> Men and Melons are hard to know. [*PRA*, Sept., 1733]

Men should do with their hopes as they do with tame fowl, cut their wings that they may not fly over the wall. [Halifax, *Moral*, p. 237]

Cut the Wings of your Hens and Hopes, lest they lead you a
weary Dance after them. [*PRA*, Feb., 1754]

Having early achieved a flexible command of the English sentence, Franklin knows how to refine the syntax of his source and
make it more euphonious.

Who goes far to marry, either goes to deceive, or to be deceived.
[Howell, *Sp. Prov.*, p. 13]
He that goes far to marry, will either deceive or be deceived.
[*PRA*, Mar., 1735]

Do not Do it if thou wilt not have it known. [Howell, *It. Prov.*, p. 6]
Do not do that which you would not have known. [*PRA*, Feb.,
1736]

Resolving to serve well, and at the same time to please, is generally resolving to do what is not to be done. [Halifax, *Polit.*, p. 215]
To serve the Publick faithfully, and at the same time please it
entirely, is impracticable. [*PRA*, Oct., 1758]

The skill with which Franklin shaped his proverbial borrowings suggests that by the time he launched the *Almanack,* in his
twenty-seventh year, he was on his way to becoming one of the
great makers of the English sentence. Whereas proverbs merely
serve to fill up the spaces in the almanacs, in his letters public
and private and in the *Autobiography* they form an integral part
of the work. Franklin's proverbial manner of expression was undoubtedly one reason the genteel critic Joseph Dennie charged
him with being "the founder of that Grubstreet sect, who have
professedly attempted to degrade literature to the level of vulgar
capacities, and debase the polished and current language of
books, by the vile alloy of provincial idioms, and colloquial barbarism, the shame of grammar, and akin to any language, rather
than English."[16] As a Boston critic had deplored the plain prose
of the *Dogood* papers, so Dennie's social bias ruled out proverbial
expression. How infinitely poorer and less idiosyncratic Franklin's style would be without it!...

In 1792, the year Robert Bailey Thomas launched the now
famous *Farmer's Almanac,* Reverend William Smith praised *Poor
Richard's Almanack* as "the Farmer's Philosopher, the Rural

[16] *The Port Folio* (Philadelphia), I (Feb. 14, 1801), 54.

Sage, the Yeomens' and Peasants' Oracle."[17] Among the countless almanacs that flourished in colonial times Franklin's stands in the first rank, both for the matter that Smith admired and for its manner of expression. No other American philomath created and developed within his pages such original types as Richard and Bridget Saunders; in subtlety no other equaled Franklin's hoax on Titan Leeds. Although Moses Coit Tyler has called Nathaniel Ames's *Astronomical Diary and Almanack* (1726-1764) "in most respects better than Franklin's,"[18] the best that can be said for it is that it had a much larger subscription.[19] Certainly Ames's sayings fall short of Franklin's in respect to perspicuity, elegance, and cadence. What finally assured the general excellence and favorable reception of *Poor Richard* is the fact that here, as on so many later occasions, Franklin seems to be relaxing after the day's labor and enjoying himself.

[17]*Eulogium on Benjamin Franklin*...(Philadelphia, 1792), p. 20, quoted in C.E. Jorgenson, *New England Quarterly*, VIII (1935), 556.

[18]Tyler, *A History of American Literature, 1607-1765* (New York, 1878), II, 122.

[19]According to Samuel Briggs, Ames's *Almanack* had an annual circulation of 60,000 copies in the period 1726-1764: *The Essays, Humor, and Poems of Nathaniel Ames,* ed. Samuel Briggs (Cleveland, 1891), p. 20n.

The Public Writings and the Bagatelles

by J.A. Leo Lemay

The Public Writings

In only one month (January 1766) Franklin wrote nine essays and satires which appeared in English periodicals, besides drafting a long pamphlet against the Stamp Act. He was the most prolific American propagandist during the pre-Revolutionary period. During the Revolution, when his time was taken up with numerous official duties, he continued to write American propaganda; and his efforts were so distinctive and superior that contemporary English writers, like Horace Walpole, could correctly identify as his the best pseudonymous pro-American writings. Throughout his life, he amused himself and others by writing satires, essays, and hoaxes—from the brief, often bawdy, mock news items in the early issues of the *Pennsylvania Gazette* to his vicious satire against slavery, written shortly before his death in 1790. Among the best of his pre-Revolutionary public writings are the free-verse satire published on June 1, 1747, of an illogical speech by the governor of Virginia concerning a fire that burned the capitol in Williamsburg; a hoax, "Rattlesnakes for Felons," May 11, 1751, in which he proposed sending rattlesnakes to England as "the most *suitable Returns*" for the convicts transported to America; his "Defense of the Americans," May 9, 1759, probably the best colonial essay on the American character (the *Papers of Benjamin Franklin* does not note that it was twice reprinted in America: in the *Boston Evening Post* for October 1 and 8, and in the *New American Magazine* for September 1759, pp. 607-13); his hoax "Of the Meanes of Disposing the Enemie to Peace," August 13, 1761, supposedly reprinting an excerpt from a treatise by a seventeenth-century Spanish priest; and his impassioned pamphlet defending the Indians from the blood-thirsty frontiersmen, *A Narrative of the Late Massacres* (1764).

Franklin's spoof of the exaggerations and absurdities of the English newspaper accounts of America, written on May 20, 1765, uses the tradition of the travel-burlesques to create the best tall tales of colonial America. He mocks the English fears of American wool production by writing: "The very Tails of the American Sheep are so laden with Wool, that each has a Car or Waggon on four little Wheels to support and keep it from trailing on the Ground. Would they caulk their Ships? would they fill their Beds? would they even litter their Horses with Wool, if it was not both plenty and cheap?" And he burlesques the unbelievable reports of American manufacturing and fishing:

And yet all this is as certainly true as the Account, said to be from Quebec, in the Papers of last Week, that the Inhabitants of Canada are making Preparations for a Cod and Whale Fishery this Summer in the Upper Lakes. Ignorant People may object that the Upper Lakes are fresh, and that Cod and Whale are Salt-water Fish: But let them know, Sir, that Cod, like other Fish, when attacked by their Enemies, fly into any Water where they think they can be safest; that Whales, when they have a mind to eat Cod, pursue them wherever they fly; and that the grand Leap of the Whale in that Chace up the Fall of Niagara is esteemed by all who have seen it, as one of the finest Spectacles in Nature![1]

Like Americans before and after him, Franklin uses tall tales to burlesque the preconceptions of his audience — and to show them how ridiculous their notions are. Those who were taken in by the tall tales only demonstrated their own incredible provinciality and ignorance.

Perhaps the best known of all the pre-Revolutionary political

[1]*The Papers of Benjamin Franklin,* ed. Leonard W. Labaree et al. (New Haven: Yale University Press, 1959-), 12: 134-35.

satires is "An Edict by the King of Prussia." Franklin wrote his son, William, an account of the reception of the "Edict." During a brief summer vacation in 1773, Franklin visited the country home of Sir Francis Dashwood, Baron Le Despencer, a notorious rake and joint Postmaster General of England. He was there when his satire was published. When the mail arrived, Paul Whitehead, himself a poet and man of letters, who customarily scanned the papers and reported to Lord Le Despencer and his guests anything remarkable, glanced through the papers "in another room, and we were chatting in the breakfast parlour, when he came running in to us, out of breath, with the paper in his hand. Here! says he, here's news for ye! *Here's the King of Prussia, claiming a right to this kingdom!* All stared, and I as much as anybody; and he went on to read it."

The analogy for the "Edict" evidently occurred to Franklin in January 1766, while he was making notes for a pamphlet against the Stamp Act. In the fifth section, after making a series of notes against the internal taxation of America, he wrote: "They [the Americans] can subsist without this Country [England] or any Trade and being too weak to express their Resentments in any other Way it will be more strongly express'd in this." Then, evidently searching for an analogy to drive home the unreasonableness of internal taxes, he wrote in the margin "Germany the Mother Country of this Nation." This inspiration contains the basic argument of the "Edict": as England is the mother country of America, so Germany is the mother country of England; just as America objects to being taxed by England, so England would object to being taxed by Germany.

The "Edict" itself is contained within the framework of an impartial persona's comment on it. The impartial observer is, significantly, a resident of Danzig (a city with a reputation for freedom and for resistance to attempted subjugation), and the account pretends to be reprinted from a Danzig newspaper. One reason for the introduction is to arouse interest in the piece, since the "Edict" itself opens with a realistic and rather dull preamble. The observer, however, begins: "We have long wondered here at the supineness of the English nation, under the Prussian impositions upon its trade entering our port." (Danzig was also famous as a free port.) Calling the English "supine" would arouse the amazement, if not the anger, of the English audience, who no doubt believed what they constantly read of English bravery, daring, and passion. It also obliquely reminds the audience (the concluding remarks do so directly) that the English reputation for intrepid action is traditionally associated with their support of freedom and liberty. The second sentence further piques the reader's curiosity, and reminds him of the English "sense of duty" and "principles of equity." The third sentence directly introduces the "Edict" and first suggests the possibility that it is a hoax.

The opening of the "Edict" itself is impersonal, formal, and realistic (quoting a portion of the supposed original French text), thereby allaying any suspicion that the document is a hoax. The second paragraph, containing the precedent, cause, and first regulation, begins by establishing the absurdly far-fetched colonial relation of England to Prussia — thus intimating that America's colonial relation to England is also exaggerated: "Whereas it is well known to all the world, that the first German settlements made in the Island of Britain, were by colonies of people, subject to our renowned ducal ancestors, and drawn from their dominions, under the conduct of Hengist, Horsa, Hella, Uff, Cerdicus, Ida, and others; and that the said colonies have flourished under the protection of our august house for ages past; have never been emancipated therefrom; and yet have hitherto yielded little profit." Franklin here slyly burlesques the arguments that America was settled at the expense of England and has been continuously dependent upon England throughout the century and a half of its existence, arguments that he elsewhere directly and repeatedly refuted. He also cleverly worked in the unworthy motive for the regulations — profit, a petty motive which will conclude the hoax and characterize (in opposition to their vainglorious opinion of themselves) the English.

The series of formal *whereas* clauses continues the parody of England's reasons for taxing America; and then, following the *therefore* clause, appears the first of the five regulations: the 4½% duty "paid to our officers of the *customs,* on all goods, wares, and merchandizes, and on the grain and other products of the earth, exported...and on all goods of whatever kind imported." The following sentence ridicules the impracticality of the duties: "that all ships or vessels bound from Great Britain to any other part of the world, or from any other part of the world to Great

Britain, shall in their respective voyages touch at our port of Koningsberg, there to be unladen, searched, and charged with the said duties." It must have been at about this point that one of the company at Lord Le Despencer's broke in on Paul Whitehead's reading with "Damn his impudence, I dare say, we shall hear by next post that he is upon his march with one hundred thousand men to back this." Readers were taken in, Franklin explained to his son, partly because of the reputation of the king of Prussia. No doubt enjoying the reactions of Lord Le Despencer's party almost as much as he had the reading and comments of the *Courant* wits on his first Silence Dogood essay, Franklin remained quiet and solemn.

The next regulation dealt with the laws regarding the mining and manufacturing of iron, Franklin parodying the common argument that the colonists must have learned mining and manufacturing from England. The irony becomes savage when Franklin indirectly states what he evidently considered the proper attitude, in one of the few passages of the "Edict" that has no counterpart in the actual British law: "and the inhabitants of the said island, presuming that they had a natural right to make the best use they could of the natural [the *natural right* brings to mind the "natural rights" philosophy, and the repeated *natural* underscores the unnaturalness of the English laws] productions of their country for their own benefit, have not only built furnaces for smelting the said stone into iron, but have erected plating-forges, slitting-mills, and steel-furnaces." These are all forbidden. "But we are nevertheless graciously [royal edicts, like Parliamentary laws, have delicious ironic possibilities] pleased to permit the inhabitants...to transport their iron into Prussia, there to be manufactured, and to them returned; they paying our Prussian subjects for the workmanship, with all the costs of commission, freight, and risk, coming and returning." It was probably at about this point that Paul Whitehead, reading the "Edict" aloud to Lord Le Despencer's group, "began to smoke it, and looking in my face said, *I'll be hanged if this is not some of your American jokes upon us.*"

The third regulation prohibits "not only the manufacturing of woollen cloth, but also the raising of wool." Franklin parodied this and emphasized its unreasonableness by implying that it violated the Americans' sacred rights of property (on which, ac-

cording to Locke, civilization is founded), by humorously cataloging the woolen goods, and by minutely specifying the ways
and places that wool could not be transported:

> and that those islanders may be farther and more effectually re-
> strained in making any advantage of their own wool in the way of
> manufacture, we command that none shall be carried out of one
> country into another; nor shall any worsted, bay, or woollen yarn,
> cloth, says, bays, kerseys, serges, frizes, druggets, cloth-serges,
> shalloons [although all these articles are listed in the original law,
> Franklin has changed their order to emphasize the rhymes and the
> incongruous awkward parechesis], or any other drapery stuffs,
> or woollen manufactures whatsoever, made up or mixed with wool
> in any of the said counties, be carried into any other county, or be
> waterborne even across the smallest river or creek on penalty of
> forfeiture of the same, together with the boats, carriages, horses,
> &c., that shall be employed in removing them.[2]

At the end of the regulations on wool, Franklin suddenly turns
scurrilous: his purpose was not only to reveal the true outrage
that Americans felt at these unjust laws, but also to show that the
laws were such serious infringements of the rights of individuals
and of countries that they could not ultimately be regarded with
the comparatively light humor which had so far characterized the
hoax. In addition, the scurrility lets the reader know that the
piece is a hoax: "Nevertheless, our loving subjects there are here-
by permitted (if they think proper) to use all their wool as manure
for the improvement of their lands."

The fourth regulation, against "the art and mystery of making
hats" is copied almost exactly from the Parliamentary statute. So
ridiculous, implies Franklin, is it, that in itself it arouses humor
and seems a parody. He adds that the "islanders...being in
possession of wool, beaver and other furs, have presumptously
[this is a word that Franklin was especially sensitive to, as the
second paragraph of the *Autobiography* shows, for he had repeatedly been accused of *presumption* in designing a lightning rod,
which would avert the just and natural punishment of God]
conceived they had a right to make some advantage thereof."
This regulation ironically concludes: "But, lest the said islanders

[2]Benjamin Franklin, *Representative Selections,* ed. Frank Luther Mott and
Chester E. Jorgenson (1935: New York: Hill and Wang, 1962), p. 361. Subsequent
references will be incorporated into the text.

[repeatedly calling the English *islanders* is itself a form of meiosis] should suffer inconveniency by the want of hats, we are farther graciously pleased to permit them to send their beaver furs to Prussia; and we also permit hats to be made thereof to be exported from Prussia to Britain; the people thus favoured to pay all costs and charges of manufacturing, interest, commission to our merchants, insurance and freight going and returning, as in the case of iron."

The last regulation echoed Franklin's earlier satires on England's sending criminals ("thieves, highway and street robbers, house-breakers, forgerers, murderers, s-d—tes, and villains of every description") to America, "for the better [!] peopleing of that country." In the penultimate paragraph of the supposed "Edict," Franklin makes the satire inescapably clear by pointing out that these "royal regulations and commands will be thought just and reasonable by our much favoured colonists" because they are "copied from their statutes" made "for the good government of their *own colonies in Ireland and America."*

The last paragraph, the penalty for disobedience, contains the final outrage—once again based on England's laws—that any persons suspected of disobeying these unreasonable and impractical laws "shall be transported in fetters from Britain to Prussia, there to be tried and executed [note that there is no possibility of being found innocent] according to the Prussian law." Had Franklin's satire closed after the dating and signature of the mock "Edict," it could still have been regarded as a *jeu d'esprit,* rather than as a serious protest and vicious condemnation of the petty, commercial self-interest that was depriving a people of their natural rights and even of the fundamentals of civilization. This, of course, is part of what Franklin added by ending the satire with the comment of the supposedly impartial Danzig observer:

> Some take this Edict to be merely one of the King's *Jeux d'Esprit* [for the final time, Franklin tells the reader it is a hoax—and offers one way to regard it] : others suppose it serious, and that he means a quarrel with England [just as every Englishman knew that if the Prussian king were to try to enforce such regulations, it must mean war, so too Franklin implies that these regulations against America will lead to war] ; but all here think the assertion it concludes with, 'that these regulations are copied from acts of the English parlia-

ment respecting their colonies,' a very injurious one; it being impossible to believe, that a people distinguished for their love of liberty, a nation so wise, so liberal in its sentiments, so just and equitable towards its neighbors, should, from mean and injudicious views of petty immediate profit, treat its own children in a manner so arbitrary and tyrannical! (*Representative Selections*, p. 363)

Thus Franklin ends the satire by reminding the English readers of their reputation for love of liberty and justice, by having the impartial persona refuse to believe that the English could have such blatantly unjust regulations, by reiterating that the motive for these acts is "mean and injudicious views of petty immediate profit," and by slyly characterizing the English as really "arbitrary and tyrannical." Although the observer seems inconsistent, for he opened the piece by describing the English as supine and closes it by echoing the traditional English self-congratulatory compliments, there is (in addition to the obvious literary reasons for the inconsistency) a level of consistency which the sensitive English reader must appreciate: in view of the existence of such regulations, the lovers of liberty and justice in England are supine—and the petty, greedy, materialists hold sway.

Franklin wrote to his son: "Lord Mansfield, I hear, said of it, that it was *very able and very artful indeed;* and would do mischief by giving here a bad impression of the measures of government; and in the colonies, by encouraging them in their contumacy." As George Simson has pointed out, the "Edict" itself follows the traditional form of the English statute: introduction (first paragraph), precedent, cause (*whereas* clauses), regulation, and penalty (last paragraph). The impartial persona framework adds a brilliant setting and interpretation of the satire, and the reversal in the conclusion (when the Danzig observer finds the assertion impossible to believe) is a microcosm of the reversal that has gone on throughout the "Edict."

The Bagatelles

Eighteenth-century men of letters sometimes wrote *jeux d'esprit* for their own amusement or for a select circle of friends. Many bagatelles ultimately had a wide circulation, because the author would allow special friends to make a copy, and they, in turn, might also give copies. Thus Franklin gave a copy of his Biblical hoax "A Parable against Persecution" to Ezra Stiles, and Stiles, on August 2, 1755, sent a copy to another literary friend. Several years later, Franklin recited it to a group of Scottish friends and was importuned for a copy by Lady Dick, which he subsequently sent; and Lord Kames asked for it in 1760, which Franklin also gave. Without asking Franklin's permission, Lord Kames promptly published it in his *Introduction to the Art of Thinking* (1761); and several years later William Strahan published a slightly different version in the *London Chronicle* for April 17, 1764, prefacing it with an amusing account of how the author, a certain North American, well-known for his "sallies of humour, in which he is a great master," would, in the middle of a conversation on the topic, get his Bible and read (that is recite from memory) this "Chapter" of Genesis. The Biblical imitation slyly burlesques Biblical morality (Abraham and his descendants will be afflicted for four hundred years because of his minor transgression), ridicules Biblical accuracy (the stranger is 198 years old), and satirizes the Scripturians who are taken in by the hoax. The parable directly recommends toleration, for if the omnipotent and omniscient creator allows various religions (and atheism) to exist, man should not object. Only six months before he died, Franklin wrote to Benjamin Vaughan of the parable: "The publishing of it by Lord Kames, without my consent, deprived me of a good deal of amusement, which I used to take in reading it by heart out of my Bible, and obtaining the remarks of the Scripturians upon it, which were sometimes very diverting; not but that it is in itself, on account of the importance of its moral, well worth being made known to all mankind."

The first of Franklin's bagatelles to be published was "The Speech of Miss Polly Baker," which mysteriously appeared in a London newspaper on April 15, 1747. It was reprinted in dozens of newspapers and magazines in England, the Continent, and America. The best text (I make this judgment for literary reasons that lack of space forbids me to spell out here) of this rhetorical tour de force appeared in the *Maryland Gazette* in the summer of 1747, from a copy in the possession of Jonas Green or some other member of Dr. Alexander Hamilton's Annapolis literary circle. This entertaining and complex hoax satirizes

New England's blue laws, protests the double-standard for women, defends prostitution, ridicules traditional Christian morality, pleads for a separation of church and state, praises philoprogenitiveness, and elegantly but subtly advocates deism. In its use of the traditional Aristotelian artificial proofs (ethos, pathos, and logos), this speech stands with the rhetorical masterpieces of the eighteenth century — and is indebted to one of them, Swift's *Modest Proposal.*

The earliest of Franklin's extant bagatelles is "Old Mistresses Apologue," dated June 25, 1745, and better known under the descriptive title "Reasons for Prefering an Old Mistress to a Young One." Although several contemporary manuscript copies survive, this *jeu d'esprit* was not popularly printed until the twentieth century. The key reason for its extraordinary success is the amazing metamorphosis in persona and tone: it begins with serious, almost stern advice being given by an elderly, kind father figure, who changes (as the basic proposition is given and the eight climactically ordered, relentless reasons are methodically stated) to an exuberant, lecherous hedonist, using a demonic, energetic tone, to a satyr who satiates and surfeits the sexual desires of his partners, before subsiding in the concluding sentence back to the original persona and tone.

Other bagatelles include his letter against attacking religion, December 13, 1757; a mock petition to the House of Commons, April 1766, on sending felons to America; the "Craven Street Gazette," September 22-26, 1770; and a great outpouring from his French period, beginning with the "Model of a Letter of Recommendation," April 2, 1777. The more famous ones are "The Flies" (propositioning Madame Brillon); "The Elysian Fields" (proposing marriage — or at least an affair — to Madame Helvetius); "Morals of Chess"; "The Whistle"; "Dialogue between Franklin and the Gout"; "The Handsome and the Deformed Leg" (an archetypal story of the optimist and pessimist); "On Wine" (burlesquing the teleological argument for the existence of God); and the scurrilous "Letter to the Academy at Brussels" (better known as "An Essay on Perfumes"). All of these — and others — are delights, but none is more delightful than "The Ephemera."

Dated "Passy Sept. 20, 1778," "The Ephemera" begins as a letter to a "dear Friend," recalling "that happy Day" spent "in the delightful Garden and sweet Society of the Molin Joli."³ The intimate and nostalgic recollection of past pleasures (with perhaps a suggestion of the Edenic joys of the Garden, joys now lost) will be the dominant tone. The second sentence indirectly introduces thoughts of death and the brevity of life: "We had been shewn numberless Skeletons of a kind of little Fly, called an Ephemere all whose successive Generations we were told were bred and expired within the Day." Then Franklin nudges the bagatelle into a childlike world of fancy, while spoofing his own absorption in natural science: "You know I understand all the inferior Animal Tongues," and makes himself more human by mocking his own poor French: "my too great Application to the Study of them is the best Excuse I can give for the little Progress I have made in your charming Language." When he writes that a "living Company" of ephemera on a leaf were "in their national Vivacity" speaking "three or four together," he suggests that there are nations of ephemera as well as of men (thereby reinforcing the microcosm/macrocosm motif) and he lightly ridicules, while characterizing, the French. "I found, however, by some broken Expressions that I caught now & then, they were disputing warmly the Merit of two foreign Musicians, one a *Cousin,* the other a *Musketo;* in which Dispute they spent their time seemingly as regardless of the Shortness of Life, as if they had been Sure of living a Month." This sentence first clearly expresses the *tempus fugit* theme, and introduces a hint of pathos, while commenting on the vanity and shallowness of most human pursuits, including the current argument over the merits of Gluck and the German school of music versus Piccini and the Italian school (implicitly comparing them to the buzzing of two similar mosquitoes is a brilliant meiosis). The emphatic conclusion of the sentence brings home both the pathos of the shortness of life and the microcosm motif. In the remainder of the introduction to the soliloquy of the "old greyheaded" ephemera, Franklin compliments the French government, proclaims himself a devotee of the "heavenly Harmony" of Madame Brillon, and playfully calls attention to the diction by the polyptoton, *amus'd, amuse,* and *Amusements.*

³Quotations are from the text published by Gilbert Chinard, "Random Notes on Two 'Bagatelles,'" *Proceedings of the American Philosophical Society,* 103 (1959), 727-60. Subsequent references will be incorporated into the text.

The ephemera's soliloquy opens:

> It was, says he, the Opinion of learned Philosophers of our Race,
> who lived and flourished long before my time, that this vast World,
> the *Moulin Joli,* could not itself subsist more than 18 Hours; and I
> think there was some Foundation for that Opinion, since by the ap-
> parent Motion of the great Luminary that gives Life to all Nature,
> and which in my time has evidently declin'd considerably towards
> the Ocean at the End of our Earth, it must then finish its Course,
> be extinquish'd in the Waters that surround us, and leave the World
> in Cold and Darkness, necessarily producing universal Death and
> Destruction. (Chinard, p. 741)

Franklin emphasizes the macrocosm/microcosm theme by having
the ephemera call the Moulin Joli, which is a small island in the
river Seine, "this vast World," and by calling the river "the Ocean
at the End of our Earth." The latter phrase, which suggests the
ancient idea of a flat earth, is in keeping with the address to the
Sun as god, for these are both characteristic beliefs of ancient
men "who lived and flourished long before." The sentence says
too that the universe we see reflects the limitations, the viewpoint, and the preconceptions of the observer and strongly suggests that a philosophy of relativism may be the most certain
truth. Franklin mocks "the Opinion of learned Philosophers of
our Race," especially those of the past, but he also implies that
the present philosophers, including, of course, himself, will have
their errors exposed in the future. And the sentence ridicules
millenarianism.

After several brief sentences on his age and the passing generations (thus reminding the reader that time is relative), the
ephemera plaintively asks "What now avails all my Toil and
Labour in amassing Honey-Dew on this Leaf, which I cannot
live to enjoy! What the political Struggles I have been engag'd in
for the Good of my Compatriotes, Inhabitants of this Bush, or my
philosophical Studies for the Benefit of our Race in general!"
In comparing a bush to a nation, Franklin again employs the
microcosm motif to stress relativism. The thought progresses
from the selfish accumulation of wealth, to political services for
the good of one's countrymen, to philosophical studies for the
benefit of mankind—but none are of any help to a dying ephemera, for there is no absolute, no final system of value inherent

in them. "For in Politics *what can Laws do without Morals.**"
Franklin notes at the bottom of the page, "*Quid leges sine mori-
bus. Hor." The classical reference, and especially calling the
reader's attention to the fact that it is a classical allusion, affirms
the cyclic, repetitive patterns of life, and indirectly argues that the
"Opinion of learned Philosophers of our Race, who lived and
flourished long before" are useful, at least in their art, and in their
expression of the basic truths of human experiences. The ephemera continues: "our present Race of Ephemeres will in a Course
of Minutes, become corrupt like those of other and older Bushes,
and consequently as wretched." Here the primitivistic persona
seems to reveal his American identity (his is a new country), as
well as his pessimism concerning the future. The ephemera implies that nations, like individuals, go through a predetermined
cycle, "And in Philosophy how small our Progress! Alas, *Art is
long and Life is short!†*" Franklin footnotes "†Hippocrates,"
again stressing the present truth of ancient thoughts and experiences. "—My Friends would comfort me with the Idea of a
Name they Say I shall leave behind me; and they tell me I have
lived long enough, to Nature and to Glory.#" For the final time,
Franklin notes the classical allusion "#Caesar." This progression
represents the time-worn channel for thoughts of mortality (and
possible immortality) to take. The persona logically, if nihilis-
tically, continues "—But what will Fame be to an Ephemere who
no longer exists? And what will become of all History in the 18th
Hour, when the World itself, even the whole *Moulin Joli* shall
come to its End, and be buried in universal Ruin?" In the return
to the ephemera's opening thought, there is no longer any strong
ridicule of the idea of millenarianism, which was a dominant element in the opening. Instead, the keynote is the fraility and
limitations of man, who has been thinking, feeling, fearing, and
saying the same things at the thought of death since at least the
flourishing of Greece and Rome. An undercurrent implies that
man, because of the limitations of his viewpoint, cannot know the
nature of death and that his ideas of it may be as fallacious as the
notion that universal ruin will come with the sunset. At the same
time, the sentence questions any doctrine of eschatology, for all
of them but reflect the limitations of the observer. The concluding sentence of the soliloquy (and the bagatelle) abandons philo-

sophical speculation and possible nihilistic thoughts to return to the "solid Pleasures" of reminiscence, social intercourse, flirtation, and art. "—To me, after all my eager Pursuits, no solid Pleasures now remain, but the Reflection of a long Life spent in meaning well, the sensible Conversation of a few good Lady-Ephemeres, and now and then a kind Smile and a Tune from the ever-amiable BRILLANTE."

The structure is deceptively simple: an introduction containing the setting and occasion, creating a special persona for Franklin, setting the tone, and suggesting the major themes; followed by the soliloquy, which stresses the cyclic structure, for we are reminded of the cycles of minutes and hours, of the life cycle of the ephemera (the speaker has "seen generations born, flourish, and expire"), and especially of the cycles of the sun. In the introduction, Franklin brought up, and stressed by its position, the word *month*. Units of cyclic (and relative) time are deliberately emphasized. Also, the reader is always conscious that Franklin is applying the fable to his own life and to the cycles of human life. The reference to "learned Philosophers...who lived and flourished long before my time," the classical allusions, and the introduction of the cyclical theory of the rise and fall of nations — all restate the cyclical theme. Moreover, the soliloquy in great part repeats and draws out the inferences and themes of the introduction, while the last sentence almost directly repeats Franklin's sentiments from the opening. Indeed, so strong is the tendency to view the concluding sentence as a return to Franklin's voice, that no present college text of "The Ephemera" prints it as part of the soliloquy, which it is.

The cyclic structure (including the two cycles of thought in the two paragraphs of the fable) subtly affirms the main theme: all life is cyclic process. The individual's participation in the process is an integral part of the whole, and possibly the individual will reappear in the cycle in the future. The structure; Franklin's persona (the friend of Madame Brillon, the lover of gardens and society, the scientist and poor student of French, the lover of music) and that of the philosopher-ephemera; the reminiscent and intimate tone with its light touch of pathos; the complexity of thought and intimation, but within a logical and time-honored progression; the ordered syntax and simple, yet connotative and precise diction—all make "The Ephemera" a brief but glorious work of art. And this is what remains above relativism; the thought of a "long Life spent in meaning well," the enjoyment of friendships, playful flirtation, and art.

Franklin's Legacy To The Gilded Age

by Louis B. Wright

For the past two centuries, Benjamin Franklin's homely aphorisms and observations have influenced more Americans than the learned wisdom of all the formal philosophers put together. From 1732, when Franklin first published his famous almanac under the pseudonym of Richard Saunders, down to the present day, the sayings of Poor Richard have entertained and instructed literally millions of readers. Since 1791, when a French translation of the first part of the "Autobiography" was published in Paris, Franklin's own narrative of his early life has been in circulation in a variety of texts. His philosophy as revealed in the Almanacs and the "Autobiography" has passed into the common stock of American thought and become the property of the multitude. His wisdom is as fresh today as it was in the eighteenth century; parents quote him to their children; editors choose from him texts for leading articles and print his proverbs as "fillers"; his remarks appear in trade journals, in advertisements, on the radio, in inspirational lectures, and even in sermons. Since his own day he has been the accepted and approved spokesman of the business man's creed—the voice and oracle of the bourgeoisie.

During the industrial and commercial expansion after the Civil War—Mark Twain's "Gilded Age"—the emphasis upon material success reached a high point of stridency. Handbooks and manuals pointing out the highroad to prosperity flourished as never before. Book agents invaded every village and hamlet, even on the most distant frontier, with prospectuses of books guaranteed to supply axioms conducive to prosperity. If any

"Franklin's Legacy to the Gilded Age." From *Virginia Quarterly Review*, 22 (1946), 268-79. Copyright 1946 by *Virginia Quarterly Review*. Reprinted by permission of *Virginia Quarterly Review* and Louis B. Wright.

youth of the Gilded Age failed to achieve a position of wealth and eminence, it was not for lack of printed advice—much of it quoted, adapted, or shamelessly plagiarized from the eighteenth-century sage.

The crassness of the materialistic advice in many of these handbooks to success would have dismayed Franklin, who believed, and demonstrated in his own career, that the mere accumulation of property was not a sufficient end in itself. Nevertheless, he had put together a vast body of pragmatic aphorisms in understandable and colloquial idiom, and the second half of the nineteenth century felt no compunction in making him the author of its favorite gospel. As the devil is said to quote Scripture to his purpose, so Jay Gould or Daniel Drew could always find a text in Franklin to fit their occasions.

Although the nineteenth century was not aware of the connection, Franklin was the link which joined the industrial and commercial spirit of that age with the ideas of the distant past when English commerce began its modern expansion. Franklin's doctrines can be found almost verbatim in the sermons and essays of scores of preachers who edified London merchants at the end of the sixteenth and the beginning of the seventeenth century. These ministers, Anglicans and Puritans alike, stressed the value of observing the prudential virtues of sobriety, diligence, and thrift. The glory of labor for its own sake became a cardinal principle of doctrine. Idleness, the preachers said, was sin, and the waste of God's precious time led inevitably to disaster in this world and damnation in the next. Protestant asceticism took the form, not of retirement from the world, but of avoidance of all those temptations and habits which wasted time and energy which ought to be devoted to the practice of one's calling. And every citizen, as the Scriptures clearly stated, must have a calling and must labor in it. These principles were the essence of a social dogma preached by the Protestant clergy of the sixteenth and seventeenth centuries.

II

Near the beginning of the present century, a German scholar, Max Weber, propounded a famous thesis which attributed much of the development of modern capitalism to Protestant ethics, particularly to the doctrines of Calvin. Characteristically Weber pushed his theories too far, for capitalism would have developed without benefit of John Calvin, but Weber's thesis had in it more than a little truth. If Protestant asceticism did not produce capitalism, it nevertheless provided an ethical code which guaranteed success to many an incipient capitalist. Given a modest break of luck, almost any intelligent youth who heeded the clergy's advice to stick to his job, stay sober, waste neither time nor money, and invest his savings thriftily, would get ahead in the world. There was scarcely anything else for him to do.

The gospel of sobriety, diligence, and thrift, transmitted to the English colonies in the seventeenth century, quickly bore fruit. With a new continent before them, zealous practicers of the prudential virtues could hardly fail. Puritans in New England and Anglicans in Virginia read many of the same sermons, heeded the advice, and soon found themselves prosperous.

Widest read of all the preachers who influenced colonial Americans was the Reverend William Perkins, who made his reputation at Cambridge in the late years of Queen Elizabeth's reign. Although he sympathized with many of the Puritan contentions, he lived and died in good standing within the Established Church. For a hundred years his published sermons and treatises were read on both sides of the Atlantic. One of his most significant works was an essay entitled "A Treatise of Vocations," first printed in 1603, which contained ideas and observations which Franklin could approve.

In fact, from Perkins directly, or from similar ideas in other preachers, or from Cotton Mather's thinly disguised adaptations of Perkins, Franklin borrowed a considerable part of his philosophy of work.

These preachments were among the first lessons that Franklin heard as a boy in Boston, and his absorption and later promulgation of the doctrines made the worldly Franklin of the eighteenth century sound much like the preachers of the seventeenth. When A. Whitney Griswold included Franklin as a Puritan in his stimulating essay entitled "Three Puritans on Prosperity," a few Franklin scholars raised their eyebrows and one complained that he would like to know "by what right Franklin is dubbed 'the soul of Puritanism.'" The evidence is clear to anyone who reads the

parsons of the age preceding Franklin's. Moreover, as Mr. Griswold shows, Franklin visited the aged Cotton Mather and
modelled some of his own first efforts in essay-writing on Mather's
work. The only plausible complaint against Mr. Griswold's clas-
sification is that the Puritans were not alone in their advocacy of
the ascetic code that guided so many men along the road to
material success. Perhaps it would be safer to describe Franklin as the authentic echo in the eighteenth century of a chorus of
advice uttered by the Protestant clergy in Elizabethan and Stuart
England.

The doctrines of the seventeenth century transmitted via
Boston, reinforced by the common sense and thrift of Quaker
ideas in Philadelphia, gave Franklin a background of bourgeois
philosophy which he expressed most completely in the sayings of
Poor Richard and in the "Autobiography."

The best epitome of Franklin's advice on how to get ahead in
the world was compiled by himself in 1757 for the Almanac of
1758 and is known as "The Speech of Father Abraham," or by its
more usual title, "The Way to Wealth." Few if any other writings
by an American have been so widely disseminated and so often
quoted. Under the fiction of an old man delivering an impromptu
bit of advice at an auction sale, Franklin gathered up his best
proverbs and wove them into a fable full of sly humor and shrewd
counsel. There, crystallized for all time, are adages which are
still commonplaces in American thinking: "Early to bed and
early to rise makes a man healthy, wealthy, and wise. ... Industry
need not wish. ... At the working man's house, Hunger looks in
but dares not enter. ... God gives all things to Industry; then
plough deep while sluggards sleep. ... Sloth, like rust, consumes
faster than labor wears; while the used key is always bright. ...
The sleeping fox catches no poultry. ... Three removes is as bad
as a fire. ... Keep thy shop and thy shop will keep thee. ... A
ploughman on his legs is higher than a gentleman on his knees. ...
Pride breakfasted with Plenty, dined with Poverty, and supped
with Infamy. ... The second vice is lying, the first is running into
debt. ... 'Tis hard for an empty meal bag to stand upright." These
proverbs and many others in the same crisp idiom are a part of
the little narrative of Father Abraham's speech, which warns near
the end that "this doctrine, my friends, is Reason and Wisdom;
but after all, do not depend too much upon your own Industry,

and Frugality, and Prudence, though excellent things, for they all may be blasted without the blessing of Heaven; and therefore ask that blessing humbly, and be not uncharitable to those that at present seem to want it, but comfort them. Remember, Job suffered and was afterwards prosperous."

This little tract, which combined worldly prudence with a dash of piety as a proper formula for success, quickly gained an international audience. Franklin himself was astonished, and not a little proud, of its reception. As he points out in the "Autobiography," English newspapers printed it widely, householders bought broadside versions and stuck them up in their houses, the clergy and gentry distributed large quantities to their parishioners and tenants, and publishers in France brought out two translations. "In Pennsylvania, as it discouraged useless expense in foreign superfluities," Franklin observed with satisfaction, "some thought it had its share of influence in producing that growing plenty of money which was observable for several years after its publication." The popularity of "The Way to Wealth" has gathered momentum from that day to this. In 1928 Lewis J. Carey in "Franklin's Economic Views" remarked that it had been published "in most of the written languages of the world and has at the present time passed through about one thousand editions in the English and about three hundred in foreign languages." After devoting fifty-six pages to listing editions of "The Way to Wealth," Paul Leicester Ford, the bibliographer of Franklin, finally gave up and announced that it was "simply impossible to find and note all the editions." The compilation of a reasonably complete bibliography of this single tract would be a lifework.

III

So succinct a manual of success, supported by the prestige of Benjamin Franklin, appealed strongly to the Gilded Age. While printed editions of the authentic Franklin continued to roll from the press in the eighteen-seventies and eighties, canny authors adapted his wisdom in handbooks of their own. Although they often quoted Franklin as the great American sage, they frequently found it convenient to expand and dilute his wisdom and serve it up as their own.

Handbooks to success have been popular in England and America for at least three centuries, but rarely have they enjoyed such esteem as in the three decades following the Civil War. Printing houses turned them out by the thousands, and book agents hawked them through the length and breadth of the land. Manuals which combined pious admonitions, hints on etiquette and behavior, and guidance in getting ahead in the business world met with particular success. The American appetite for this type of literature was insatiable, and book agents further stimulated public taste by their own persuasions. Few families neglected to accumulate a pile of these instructive guides.

A typical example of a manual which pillaged from Franklin and attained great popularity was "Worth and Wealth. Or the Art of Getting, Saving, and Using Money," by T. L. Haines, A. M., published by Haines Brothers, Chicago, 1883. It was a stout and handsome volume, illustrated with moralistic engravings, and bound in cloth, half-leather, or full leather, depending on how much the customer wanted to spend on a gift book for his favorite son or nephew, or for a clerk who might find its lessons profitable both to himself and his employer. "Worth and Wealth" was in high favor during the eighties. The firm of Haines Brothers apparently dedicated itself almost entirely to its distribution, and from Chicago a flood of these guides poured out upon the ambitious Middle West. The book is significant of the way in which the later nineteenth century made Franklin the prophet and evangel of materialism.

Haines' compilation was original neither in its title nor its contents. More than forty years before, in 1850, Freeman Hunt, editor of the Merchants Magazine, had published "Worth and Wealth: A Collection of Maxims, Morals and Miscellanies, for Merchants and Men of Business," which had borrowed suitable aphorisms and anecdotes from Franklin and numerous other authors. When Haines came to put together his book, he appropriated Hunt's title and certain passages that suited his purposes, but Haines' "Worth and Wealth" was a new, streamlined, and up-to-date manual useful to every ambitious youth of 1883. If Haines still found Franklin's advice modern and serviceable, it merely proved the eternal wisdom of that great man.

Like scores of other success books, Haines' manual brought together a vast quantity of conventional platitudes on conduct and behavior, but a saturation in Poor Richard's sayings gave Haines a certain crispness lacking in most of his contemporaries. The chapter entitled "The Road to Riches" owes an obvious but unacknowledged debt to Franklin, and elsewhere throughout the book Haines betrays his obligation. Occasionally when he thinks that Franklin would give authority to his counsel he quotes him by name, as in the chapter on "Industry" which offers whole chunks of pragmatic advice from "The Way to Wealth."

A work which borrowed so much from Franklin ought to have reflected here and there a glint of his humor and his realization that mere acquisitiveness is not enough. But Haines was a serious, earnest man who, solemnly and sanctimoniously, preached a gospel of getting rich. His was the zeal of a crusader, and he made a religion of material success as a sufficient end in itself.

Furthermore, Haines declares in so many words that the man of business is the saint of the modern world, and his book at times becomes ecstatic as he contemplates the apotheosis of the holy men of the market place.

The opening sentences of "Worth and Wealth" state a theme which recurs in varied forms in every chapter. "Business is king," Haines announces at the start. "Other influences in society may be equally indispensable, and some may think far more dignified; but business is king. The statesman and the scholar, the nobleman and the prince, the manufacturer, the mechanic, and the laborer, pursue their several objects only by leave granted, and means furnished by this potentate." With that beginning, the reader is given to understand that the book will instruct all youths who aspire to be heirs apparent in the means of achieving their royal inheritance.

From mere earthly kingship, Haines presently leads his reader to the contemplation of a state even more sublime for the successful man of affairs. In phraseology reminiscent of King David, the author announced the canonization of the American who reaches the heights. "The saint of the nineteenth century," he asserts flatly, "is the good merchant; he is wisdom for the foolish, strength for the weak, warning to the wicked and a blessing to all. Build him a shrine in bank and church, in the market and the exchange, or build it not: no saint stands higher than this saint of trade."

The achievement of this apotheosis, this progress from king-

ship to godhead, comes through application and diligence, an
everlasting and unceasing concentration upon the duties of one's
calling. "Never be idle," Haines abjures his readers. "If your
hands cannot be usefully employed, attend to the cultivation of
your mind."

Time is money, and he who wastes God's precious time wastes
his own inheritance, Haines affirms, echoing the preachers for
three centuries. "As every thread of gold is valuable, so is every
minute of time. Cents, like minutes, are often thrown away because people do not know what to do with them," he insists. But
those with a proper sense of time's value may grow rich and great,
like Stephen Girard or Russell Sage.

Besides thrift and diligence, Haines emphasizes certain other
qualities, useful in the attainment of success, by devoting chapters
to them early in the book. Some of these virtues, as described in
the chapter headings, are business training, courtesy, system, accuracy, prudence, patience, earnestness, decision, self-depen-
dence, grit, and integrity in business. Running through all of the
work is an insistence that honesty is the best policy. Indeed, the
stress on faithfulness in keeping one's trust, especially in matters
concerned with an employer's time and money, endeared the
book to many a merchant eager to induce in his clerks a desire to
follow the paths of probity. These passages explain why presi-
dents of firms in the eighties found "Worth and Wealth" a
favored gift to bestow upon their employees in lieu of a bonus at
Christmas.

Haines is particularly eloquent upon the ultimate rewards of
dealing honestly with one's employer. Indeed, his language at-
tains a mystical and Biblical fervor in describing the reception
into heaven of the honest clerk on the Day of Judgment when at
last he will come into his own. Haines' vision of this exaltation is
one of the purplest patches in the book:

> After the last store has been closed; after the last bank has gone
> down; after the shuffle of the quick feet on the stone walks has
> stopped; after the long line of merchantmen on the seas have taken
> sail of flame; after Chicago, and New York, and London, and
> Vienna, have gone down into the grave, where Thebes, and
> Babylon, and Tyre lay buried; after the great firebells of the judg-
> ment-day have tolled at the burning of the world—on that day all
> the affairs of banking-houses and stores will come up for inspec-

tion. O what an opening of account books! Side by side the clerks and the men who employed them—the people who owned thread-and-needle stores on the same footing with the Stewarts, and the Fields, and the Claflins, and the Barings. ... That will be the great day for the honest clerk. ... They will go from glory to glory, and from song to song, and from throne to throne. While others go down into the eternal sea, with their gold like millstones hanging to their necks, they shall climb up the heights of amethyst and alabaster, holding in their right hands the pearl of great price. All the beautiful hosts of virtue will stand serenely around the throne of Almighty God, amid the smoke of firmaments and the crash of worlds.

Whether the contemplation of a seat at the right hand of Abraham—and of the Fields and the Barings—enraptured the forty-dollar-a-month clerk as much as it did the author of "Worth and Wealth," we have no way of knowing. But we are certain that thousands came into possession of the book and many of the surviving copies show evidence of diligent perusal.

IV

For the benefit of ambitious youths who required something more tangible than the hope of holding the pearl of great price in their right hands as they ascended to heaven, Haines includes near the end of his book a special chapter entitled the "Testimony of Millionaires." The sententious wisdom of such Poloniuses of commerce as Stephen Girard, Commodore Vanderbilt, Russell Sage, and John McDonogh pointed the way for others to follow in their footsteps. Here were the visible results of the whole philosophy of diligence and thrift, and here were the very words, sacred within their quotation marks, which had fallen from the lips of these demigods of the market place. They spoke like parsons, all except Stephen Girard, who cold-bloodedly asserted that labor like that of a galley-slave, without any help from on high, had produced his wealth.

Although Haines, with Emersonian faith, emphasizes the value of self-reliance, Girard went a step too far, and the author hastened to assure his readers that the Almighty had a hand in their destinies and kept a watchful eye on business. While it was true that God helped those who helped themselves, ambitious youths should remember to solicit their Creator earnestly to assist them in their endeavors. To drive home that lesson, the author concludes his testimony of millionaires with the rules of life which John McDonogh of New Orleans ordered engraved on his tombstone.

McDonogh's third rule receives special stress because of its truth and utility. "You must pray to the Almighty with fervor and zeal," Haines quotes McDonogh as saying, "and you will be sustained in all of your desires. I never prayed sincerely to God in all my life without having my prayer answered satisfactorily. Follow my advice and you will become a rich man." Many a seventeenth-century preacher, addressing London apprentices, had employed almost the same words.

So pious a lesson required comment from the author, and Haines himself duly points out that "prayer prepares the mind for great undertakings; it gives an earnestness and seriousness to the character; it curbs that levity and frivolity which trifle with important concerns, viewing everything as a game;... It invokes to human exertions the favor and influence of the Most High. God will hear and answer sincere prayer." In this fashion, "Worth and Wealth" concludes its pious admonitions of the asceticism of the Gilded Age, which had for its goal, not holiness as in the medieval world, or proof of spiritual election as with the Calvinistic Puritans, but the accumulation of this world's goods.

The bourgeois philosophy which flowered so rankly in the nineteenth century had been growing since Elizabeth was queen of England, but it remained for post-Civil War America to bring the gospel to its materialistic culmination. By a credible though partial perception of Benjamin Franklin's philosophy, the later nineteenth century made that great American its high priest of the religion of commercial success. But first it stripped him of his urbanity, his humor, his understanding of intellectual values, and his genuine wisdom. An age which was fond of quoting "A Psalm of Life" to prove that "Life is real! Life is earnest!" and we must "Learn to labor and to wait," could easily interpret Franklin through one work alone, "The Way to Wealth." By a curious irony, one of the least ascetic of Americans became the scriptural authority for the least desirable of all types of asceticism, that which ended in mere material acquisition.

Chronology of Important Dates

1706   Benjamin Franklin born January 17 (January 6, 1705/1706, Old Style) in Boston.

1718   Apprenticed to his brother James, a printer.

1722   The "Dogood Letters" appear in the *New England Courant* published by James Franklin.

1723   Runs away to Philadelphia; finds work with Samuel Keimer.

1724-26   In London; works as printer at Palmer's and Watt's.

1725   *A Dissertation on Liberty and Necessity.*

1727-36   Begins his independent career in Philadelphia. Forms the Junto; opens his own printing office and stationer's shop in partnership with Hugh Meredith; prints his pamphlet on paper currency and is appointed printer to the Pennsylvania Assembly; begins publishing *The Pennsylvania Gazette;* takes Deborah Read Rogers to wife; dissolves his partnership; founds the Library Company of Philadelphia; begins publishing *Poor Richard's Almanack* (1733-58); sees his natural son William born (1731) and his son Francis Folger born (1732) and die (1736).

1729   The "Busy-Body" Papers.

1730   "A Witch Trial at Mount Holly."

1736-56   Period of public service in Philadelphia. Appointed clerk of the Assembly; forms Union Fire Company; becomes postmaster of Philadelphia (to 1753); invents the "Franklin stove"; organizes the militia; is elected to the Philadelphia Common Council; proposes an Academy — eventually to become the University of Pennsylvania; founds the American Philosophical Society; helps charter the Pennsylvania Hospital; founds and heads the first fire insurance company; becomes joint deputy postmaster general of North America; shapes the Albany Plan of Union; raises supplies for General Braddock's expedition against the Indians.

1741   Publishes *The General Magazine.*

1743   *A Proposal for Promoting Useful Knowledge* leads to the formation of the American Philosophical Society. Daughter Sarah born.

1747   *Plain Truth.*
            "The Speech of Miss Polly Baker."

1748   Enters into partnership with David Hall and retires from active business.
            "Advice to a Young Tradesman."

1749   *Proposals Relating to the Education of Youth in Pennsylvania.*

1751-54   *Experiments and Observations on Electricity* (in three parts). *Observations Concerning the Increase of Mankind.*

1752   The kite experiment performed and published.

1753   Awarded the Copley Medal by the Royal Society for his scientific work and receives honorary M.A.s from Harvard and Yale.

1756   Elected a Fellow of the Royal Society. Receives honorary M.A. from William and Mary College.

1757-62   In England as Colonial Agent for Pennsylvania, treating with the Penn family largely on matters of taxing the Proprietors' estates.

1757   *The Way to Wealth.*

1759   The University of St. Andrews makes him "Dr. Franklin."

1760   *The Interest of Great Britain Considered.*

1762   Receives degree of Doctor of Civil Laws from Oxford. William Franklin marries and is appointed royal governor of New Jersey.

1764   *A Narrative of the Late Massacres* denounces the slaughter of friendly Indians.
            Cool Thoughts argues a change from proprietary to royal status for Pennsylvania.

1764-75   Again in England as Agent, eventually for four colonies. He defends the colonies before Parliament against the Stamp Act and gradually comes to recognize the necessity for independence.

1768	"Causes of the American Discontents Before 1768."
1771	Begins the *Autobiography*.
1773	"Rules By Which a Great Empire May Be Reduced to a Small One." "An Edict of the King of Prussia."
1774	Affair of the Hutchinson letters; dismissed as deputy postmaster general. Deborah Franklin dies in Philadelphia.
1776	Signs *The Declaration of Independence*.
1776-85	In France, originally as one of three American commissioners, later as Minister Plenipotentiary. Arranges for the French alliance (1778). Signs the Treaty of Paris (1783). Retires to Passy, where he sets up a private press. Lionized by the French throughout this period.
1778	*The Ephemera*.
1784	*Information to Those Who Would Remove to America*. Resumes his autobiography.
1785	Elected President of Pennsylvania (to 1788).
1787	Delegate to the Constitutional Convention.
1788	Retires from public life. Begins writing Part Three of his autobiography.
1790	Dies April 17.

Notes on the Editor and Contributors

BRIAN M. BARBOUR teaches at Providence College and has edited *American Transcendentalism: An Anthology of Criticism.*

CARL L. BECKER (1873-1945) taught at Cornell from 1917 until his death. His many books included *The Declaration of Independence* and *The Heavenly City of the Eighteenth-Century Philosophers.*

MICHAEL T. GILMORE teaches at Brandeis. He has edited *Twentieth Century Interpretations of Moby-Dick.*

BRUCE GRANGER teaches at the University of Oklahoma. His books include *Political Satire in the American Revolution.*

D.H. LAWRENCE (1885-1930) was the greatest English novelist of the century. His indispensable criticism can be found in the two volumes of *Phoenix* and in his *Letters.*

J.A. LEO LEMAY is the H.F. duPont Winterthur Professor of English at the University of Delaware.

DAVID LEVIN is Commonwealth Professor of English at the University of Virginia.

KENNETH S. LYNN, formerly Professor of English at Harvard, is Professor of History at Johns Hopkins. His books include *The Dream of Success* and *Visions of America.*

PERRY MILLER (1905-1963) taught at Harvard. His two volumes on *The New England Mind* revolutionized the study of American intellectual history.

DANIEL B. SHEA, JR. teaches at Washington University and has been a Fulbright lecturer at the University of Caen.

LEWIS P. SIMPSON is the William A. Read Professor of English at Louisiana State University and co-editor of *The Southern Review.*

JOHN WILLIAM WARD, President of Amherst College, has written *Andrew Jackson: Symbol For An Age.*

MAX WEBER (1864-1920) was originally an economist, but his work has profoundly influenced historical thought, the sociology of religion, sociological theory, and political science.

LOUIS B. WRIGHT was for many years Director of the Folger Shakespeare Library in Washington; he is presently Consultant in History to the National Geographic Society. His many books include *Middle Class Culture in Elizabethan England, Culture on the Moving Frontier,* and *The Cultural Life of the American Colonies.*

Selected Bibliography

I. BIBLIOGRAPHIES

There is no complete modern bibliography of or about Franklin. The most helpful bibliographical essay is by Bruce Granger in *Fifteen American Authors Before 1900*, ed. Robert A. Rees and Earl N. Harbert (Madison: University of Wisconsin Press, 1971), pp. 185-206. J.A. Leo Lemay, "Franklin and the *Autobiography:* An Essay on Recent Scholarship," *Eighteenth Century Studies,* I (December 1967), 185-211, ranges more widely than the title suggests and includes a review of the first ten volumes of the Yale edition (see Part II). For the period up to 1936 the most complete bibliography is in Chester E. Jorgenson and Frank Luther Mott, eds., *Benjamin Franklin: Representative Selections* (New York, 1936), pp. cli-clxxxviii. Richard Beale Davis, *American Literature Through Bryant,* Goldentree Bibliographies in Language and Literature (New York: Appleton-Century-Crofts, 1969), pp. 30-34, is pithy.

II. EDITIONS

The Yale edition of *The Papers of Benjamin Franklin,* ed. Leonard W. Labaree et al., 20 vols. to date (New Haven, 1959-) aims at being comprehensive. It tries to reprint both sides of Franklin's extensive correspondence, for example, and includes important "third person" documents. It is complete through 1773. For the later years the standard edition is still Albert Henry Smyth's, *The Writings of Benjamin Franklin,* 10 vols. (New York: Macmillan, 1905-7). A selective work of modern scholarship is *Benjamin Franklin's Letters to the Press, 1758-1775,* edited by Verner W. Crane (Chapel Hill: University of North Carolina Press, 1950).

The textual history of the *Autobiography* is bizarre, but Franklin's holograph is in the Huntington Library and has served as the basis for the two important modern editions. *Benjamin Franklin's Memoirs. Parallel Text Edition,* ed. Max Farrand (Berkeley: University of California Press, 1949) prints in parallel columns four texts—the Huntington manuscript, Temple Franklin's first American edition, and two French translations that were made from a copy of the manuscript Franklin sent to France in November of 1789. The format allows for easy study of changes, but the book is now out of print. *The Autobiography of Benjamin Franklin*, ed. Leonard W. Labaree et al. (New Haven: Yale University Press, 1964) is a product of the Yale edition of *The Papers*. For a discussion of the differences consult the introduction of the Yale edition. Among paperback reprints there are *Autobiography and Other Writings*, ed. Russell B. Nye (Boston: Riverside Press, 1958) with a good introduction; and *Benjamin Franklin's Autobiography and Selected Writings*, ed. Larzer Ziff (New York: Holt, Rinehart and Winston, 1959), an excellent selection.

III. BIOGRAPHY

Van Doren, Carl. *Benjamin Franklin*. New York: Viking, 1938. The standard work and, until publication of *The Papers* is complete, likely to remain so.

IV. CRITICISM

Lemay and Granger (Part I above) both provide useful surveys of the criticism. The following items have appeared since 1970; two or three older items worthy of special attention are also listed.

Brooks, Van Wyck. *America's Coming-of-Age*. New York: Dutton, 1915. Argues that American experience divides between Jonathan Edwards (the "highbrow") and Franklin (the "lowbrow") without any adequate middle ground.

England, A.B. "Some Thematic Patterns in Franklin's *Autobiography*," *Eighteenth Century Studies* 5 (Spring 1972), 421-30.

Gallagher, Edward J. "The Rhetorical Strategy of Franklin's 'Way to Wealth,'" *Eighteenth Century Studies* 6 (Spring 1973), 475-85.

Griffith, John. "The Rhetoric of Franklin's *Autobiography*," *Criticism* 13 (Winter 1971), 77-94. Highly recommended.

Griswold, A. Whitney. "Three Puritans on Prosperity," *New England Quarterly* 7 (September 1934), 475-93. The other two are Cotton Mather and Timothy Dwight; in Weber's tradition.

Halio, Jay L. "American Dreams," *Southern Review*, n.s., 13 (Autumn 1977), 837-44. Shows that the contemporary American novel is still concerned to distinguish the Franklinian and Emersonian conceptions of the American dream.

Kenney, W. Howland, ed. *Laughter in the Wilderness: Early American Humor to 1783.* Kent, Ohio: Kent State University Press, 1976.

Lawrence, D.H. *The Symbolic Meaning: The Uncollected Versions of "Studies in Classic American Literature,"* ed. Armin Arnold (London: Centaur Press, 1962). The first version of Lawrence's essay is given. It is more discursive in style, arguing the danger of Franklin's emphasis on the will.

Leary, Lewis. *Soundings: Some Early American Writers,* pp. 8-44. Athens: University of Georgia Press, 1975.

Lemay, J.A. Leo, ed. *The Oldest Revolutionary: Essays on Benjamin Franklin.* Philadelphia: University of Pennsylvania Press, 1976. Besides the piece by Lewis P. Simpson reprinted herein, see especially David L. Parker, "From Sound Believer to Practical Preparationist: Some Puritan Harmonics in Franklin's *Autobiography."*

Lynen, John F. *The Design of the Present: Essays on Time and Form in American Literature,* pp. 87-153. New Haven: Yale University Press, 1969.

Miller, Perry. *Nature's Nation.* Cambridge: Harvard University Press: The Belknap Press, 1967, pp. 208-40. Interesting discussion of Franklin and the plain style.

Murphy, Denis M. "Poor Robin and Shrewd Ben: Hawthorne's 'Kinsman,'" *Studies in Short Fiction* 15 (Spring 1978), 185-90.

Rawlinson, D.H. *The Practice of Criticism.* Cambridge: Cambridge University Press, 1968, pp. 134-40. Good commentary on Lawrence's criticism of Franklin.

Rucker, Mary E., "Benjamin Franklin," in *American Literature, 1764-1789: The Revolutionary Years,* ed. Everett Emerson. Madison: University of Wisconsin Press, 1977.

Sanford, Charles L., ed. *Benjamin Franklin and the American Character.* Problems in American Civilization. Boston: D.C. Heath, 1955.

Sappenfield, James A. *A Sweet Instruction: Franklin's Journalism as a Literary Apprenticeship.* Carbondale: Southern Illinois University Press, 1973.

Tatham, Campbell. "Benjamin Franklin, Cotton Mather, and the Outward State," *Early American Literature* 6 (Winter 1971-72), 223-33.

Wylie, Irvin G. *The Self-Made Man in America: The Myth of Rags to Riches.* New Brunswick, N.J.: Rutgers University Press, 1954. The standard work on the literature of self-improvement, which took its inspiration from Franklin.